VIOLENCE IN ARGENTINE LITERATURE

VIOLENCE IN ARGENTINE LITERATURE

CULTURAL RESPONSES TO TYRANNY

DAVID WILLIAM FOSTER

University of Missouri Press
Columbia and London

Copyright © 1995 by

The Curators of the University of Missouri

University of Missouri Press, Columbia, Missouri 65201

Printed and bound in the United States of America

5 4 3 2 1   99 98 97 96 95

Library of Congress Cataloging-in-Publication Data

Foster, David William, 1940–

   Violence in Argentine literature : cultural responses to tyranny /
David William Foster.

    p. cm.

   Includes bibliographical references (p.   ) and index.

   ISBN 0-8262-0991-2 (alk. paper)

   1. Argentine literature—20th century—History and criticism.

2. Argentine fiction—20th century—History and criticism. 3. Argentine
literature—Political aspects. 4. Violence in literature. 5. Literature
and society—Argentina. I. Title.

PQ7655.F67 1995

860.9'982—dc20   94-47196

                                              CIP

For permissions to reproduce copyrighted material, see
Acknowledgments.

∞ This paper meets the requirements of the
American National Standard for Permanence of Paper
for Printed Library Materials, Z39.48, 1984.

Designer: Stephanie Foley

Typesetter: BOOKCOMP

Printer and Binder: Thomson-Shore, Inc.

Typefaces: Antique Olive and Palatino

CONTENTS

ACKNOWLEDGMENTS

Research for this project was made possible by various grant programs of Arizona State University. Daniel Altamiranda, Roselyn Costantino, Darrell Lockhart, Melissa Lockhart, José María García Sánchez, Gustavo Geirola, and Salvador Oropesa have served as my research assistants during various stages of its preparation.

The preliminary versions of some of this material are marked by an asterisk in the Bibliography of Secondary Sources at the end of this study. Additionally, some of the comments on specific texts appeared as review notes in *World Literature Today* and *Chasqui: revista de literatura latinoamericana.*

Formal acknowledgment is made as follows for permission to quote from copyrighted material:

Passages from *The Bloody Countess* by Alejandra Pizarnik are reprinted by permission of Crown Publishers, New York. Translation copyright © 1986 by Alberto Manguel.

Passages from the author's translation of Enrique Medina's *Las tumbas (The Tombs)* are reprinted by permission of Garland Publishing, New York. Copyright © 1993.

"Identidades polimórficas y planteo metateatral en *Extraño juguete* de Susana Torres Molina" was originally published in *Alba de América,* and is reprinted in part by permission of the publisher.

"Pornography and the Feminine Erotic: Griselda Gambaro's *Lo impenetrable*" was originally published in *Monographic Review/*

Revista monográfica, and is reprinted in part by permission of the publisher.

"Traspasando los géneros literarios" was originally published in *Ideas '92,* and is reprinted in part by permission of the publisher.

VIOLENCE IN ARGENTINE LITERATURE

The words of reality are not always within our grasp, but we are able to know what they are.

(Las palabras de la realidad no están siempre a nuestro alcance, pero podemos llegar a saber cuáles son.)

—Juan Carlos Martini,
La vida entera (The whole life)

INTRODUCTION

Preliminary Considerations on the Redemocratization of Argentine Culture

Argentina returned to democracy in 1983. A process of restructuring had already begun with the call for elections in that year and with the swearing in of Raúl Alfonsín in December. Alfonsín's assumption of the presidency completed the formal transition from military tyranny to a constitutional government. This process of transition, of institutional redemocratization, involved many fundamental and radical changes, among them a reorganization of national culture to bring it into line with the provisions and safeguards for culture established in the Argentine constitution.

Many people of importance participated in the redemocratization of Argentina and its culture. The extensive list of artists, writers, and intellectuals involved attests to the broadness of the participation in the many phases of restructuring on all levels of Argentine society.

In order to speak of the redemocratization of Argentine culture, we must first consider what is meant by the word *culture*. What are the elements of national institutional life that make up the culture of a nation? We may ask ourselves, what is the relationship between the daily life of people and the elements that constitute culture? This question encompasses informal as well as formal elements of culture; elements of public life as well as of private existence; elements that receive official support as well as those that exist without any sort of official recognition or stimulus from

1

federal, provincial, or municipal governments. Argentina is a nation that has attempted historically to establish a place for itself within the framework of the Western cultural tradition and the definitions understood by this tradition. As a consequence, prevailing Argentine definitions of culture sound very much like those heard in Europe and the United States. Yet at the same time, part of the research on this topic cannot avoid concerning itself with exactly how a plural culture is maintained in a nation, especially one that has undergone a recent history like Argentina's.

Also of interest is the extent to which culture should receive official support and be tied to official and, therefore, political criteria. To put it differently, what do we mean by an official cultural policy? This is a topic that has been extensively debated in the United States.

The term *redemocratization* carries with it the implication that at some prior stage culture was not democratic and that what is involved is a return to a democratic culture. There is the further implication that at an even earlier stage culture *was* democratic and that the quality was somehow lost or suppressed. Moreover, the lexical structure of the word bespeaks a process of transformation from a nondemocratic culture to a democratized one, the *-ize* suffix being the explicit marker of this process.

What are the configurations of this process? What activities must there be to achieve such a goal? To what degree is this a self-propelling process, in which possibilities are inherent in a certain set of social and political circumstances and which is an extension of the dynamics of these circumstances by virtue of the inner logic of both culture and its wider existential setting? Or must this process be set in motion by agents of cultural change? Who, then, might these agents be? Do they belong to official circles, or do they come from the private sector? Are they the writers, artists, and intellectuals themselves, or are they the consumers of culture, who place specific demands on cultural production? In sum, wherein lies the *agentivizing* factor of cultural redemocratization?

From the point of view of a scholarly inquiry into the subject, there would seem to be three areas that require special attention.

The first area involves the recovery of the literature produced in Argentina during the period of the tyranny. There are various ways of defining this period, but for our purposes we are speaking of the eight years between 1976 and 1983, although some attention must be paid to texts from the earlier round of authoritarian regimes between 1966 and 1973: indeed, to the extent that the 1973–1976 Peronist interlude can be seen less as a stillborn attempt to return to democracy and more as a reaffirmation of political authoritarianism abetted and then taken over by the military, the entire period between 1966 and 1983 can be seen as a single cycle in Argentine social history. During this period, Argentine cultural production was continued, both by people who remained in the country and by those who, for a number of complex personal reasons, chose or were forced to work from abroad. In the case of the latter group of artists, although their production may have been performed or published outside Argentina, it was almost inevitable that their texts evinced both a specifically Argentine viewpoint conditioned by the internal affairs of their homeland and an explicit thematics as the consequence of their personal experiences.

We have a fairly complete bibliographic record of this cultural production, despite the fact that a good part of what was produced in Argentina was censored and the texts are often difficult to obtain.[1] Thus, it is possible to form an idea of what was going on in Argentina and what Argentines in exile were engaged in creating. Yet at some point it becomes important to investigate in detail all of the proportions of this culture within and against the military tyranny, and to place it within the larger framework of Argentine cultural history. It is also necessary to compare this culture with the similar and dissimilar circumstances of culture in other Latin American nations during the same period, both those experiencing dictatorship and those functioning as constitutional societies.

To study the outlines of this culture, correlate its production with what was happening within Argentina, identify it with what was happening elsewhere in Latin America, and compare it with the

1. Andrés Avellaneda, *Censura, autoritarismo y cultura.*

vision of Argentine society held by Argentines themselves both in and outside the country are necessary steps in constructing the network of social texts that give cultural meaning to the production, and to often aborted attempts at production, during the period in question. We know all too well that there was an opposition culture during this period that suffered extreme forms of censorship and repression. Yet we cannot limit ourselves only to the culture of opposition, to whatever extent we can be comfortable in delimiting it categorically.

Both the military and the many segments of society that supported it in one way or another at one time or another—the Catholic Church, the business and financial establishment, various leagues of social action, agencies of external influence—also produced an official and quasiofficial culture that must somehow be factored into any sort of satisfactory analysis. The culture of this period presents an extremely fragmented pattern, in part because culture in a dynamic society like Argentina is always going to be pulling in many different directions, although there is no escaping the fact that many of the examples of fragmentation at issue here are the consequence of the imposition of a tyrannical militarization on all of the nation's institutions.

This fragmentation concerns both the life and the production of individual writers and artists, as well as the contexts in which their work was produced, published, exhibited, distributed, and the like—in short, all of the mechanisms of censorship and repression that interrupt and block the sort of cultural life we customarily associate with a pluralistic democracy. Thus, the culture of opposition becomes a marginal and forgotten production both in its precariousness and frequent disappearance, and in the lack of the sort of secondary production of criticism that it generates in open societies as part of the widening repercussions of unfettered cultural production. To all of this must be added also the consequences of the autocensorship that arose in response to the climate of the period and which sprang from the fear that one's works would be confiscated and one punished or eliminated as the result of uncontrolled self-expression.

The second area that requires investigation concerns the reassessment of the Argentine literary tradition. It is well known that during dictatorial regimes there is a profound revisionism in academic programs and their equivalents in other sectors (such as the literary supplements of newspapers that fall into line with junta policy). Therefore, texts and other sources of information about the nation's literary traditions are seriously modified, if not directly distorted, by the imperatives of propaganda, censorship, and general cultural *sanitization.*

If what we understand by a democratic culture is the possibility of a research program that is unchecked by such considerations, the need emerges under democracy to go back to the founding texts of the cultural tradition and all of the subsequent versions of national identity in order to promote a reconstituted reading of Argentine history outside the confines of dictatorial or tyrannical interpretations. The simple fact that Argentina has made the transition to a new phase of its national life encourages such a rereading of cultural history as part of the enormously complex process of national synthesis and consensus, and it stimulates a pluralistic understanding of how Argentina as a nation has been inscribed in its cultural traditions. This involves understanding key texts and various degrees of secondary texts (and by text I do not mean to limit the matter to literature alone, but to emphasize all cultural production) in terms of the present moment, the period of military tyranny that is in the process of being left behind, the conditions that led to it, and the difficulties of sustaining a democratic culture that will help prevent the recurrence of dictatorial regimes. All of this implies a strong interest in the need to reconstruct a historical continuity for national culture via the process of reassessing prior cultural production. One very practical result of this reassessment might be an understanding of how culture has evolved in earlier periods of institutional reconstruction.

This leads to the third field of inquiry, the specifically immediate question of what forms Argentine culture has been taking during the years since redemocratization. To the extent that this is a time when Argentine culture has before it extensive opportunities to take new forms and to reach new audiences (despite continuing economic factors that do provide some very real barriers to its fullest development), it is inevitable that we inquire after specific innovations being pursued among the various sectors involved and in the various fields of activity. Are there specifically new genres and themes in Argentine culture that are the consequence of a changed perspective made possible by institutional redemocratization? While it would be naive to think in terms of radical innovations and dramatic breaks with past forms of cultural production, it is legitimate to begin such an inquiry with the assumption that the simple abolition of official censorship and the opportunity to engage in a level of freedom of expression unknown to many of the writers and artists who came to maturity during Argentina's darkest years will have produced something in the way of distinctly different cultural modalities.

The opportunity to take new and perhaps audacious positions as to what constitutes culture and what role it should play in national life cannot help but lead to the emergence of texts that would have been unthinkable ten years ago. By virtue of the fact that one of the abiding features of contemporary Western culture is a sustained vanguard mentality and the unchecked quest for new forms of expression, it would be inconceivable to believe that less than a decade has not produced anything profoundly different in the outlines of Argentine culture in response to the process of institutional redemocratization. This is particularly true if we insist on defining culture in the broadest terms possible, to include, beyond the limitations of elitist notions, all of the varieties of personal experience and reflection that go toward helping the individual meet the physical and emotional needs of daily existence. And this is also particularly true if we pursue a definition of cultural involvement that is as all-inclusive as possible in defining both the producers and the consumers of culture.

A conception of cultural text that promotes a notion of continuity among the various codes and registers of social discourse and among the multiple inscriptions assumed by this discourse is fundamental to understanding all that might actually or possibly be occurring in Argentine culture. In part, there must be an interest in which forms and acts of existence and their cultural reflexes were forbidden under the tyranny, and in how they have (re)emerged since 1983 along with what are essentially new varieties of experience that have entered the realm of cultural dynamics.

Argentina has always been a nation of enormous cultural production, even during the worst moments in its history. Therefore, it is no surprise to discover that democracy has meant a concomitant increase in an already culturally intensive society. This makes for an enormous challenge to cultural critics and historians, especially if their definitions of culture are as broad as I have suggested they must be to provide an adequate rendering of the most interesting and the most innovative phenomena in Argentine culture today. Yet it is precisely in terms of this vast array of phenomena that the most vital and significant aspects of cultural redemocratization in Argentina are to be sought.

There are three dominant perspectives regarding Argentine culture, especially as it relates to production during and after the period of authoritarianism. The first is that of the cultural producers— and their consumers—who remained in the country, adapting themselves as best they could to the often terrible circumstances of daily life, beginning with the constant, disingenuous manipulation of the news and extending to the routine underground reports of acts of aggression by the government against its citizens. The cultural production from within Argentina is indelibly marked by these circumstances, and one can reasonably be ambivalent in praising what contestatorial production did emerge while lamenting the inevitable distortions and compromises that took place, the worst of which was the practice of self-censorship.

In contrast, the large number of exiled writers, intellectuals, and artists constituted a sort of external Argentine culture. This production is in a very real sense continuous with the internal production (certainly, it is thematically marked by an almost obsessive focus on interpreting life under the military tyranny from the vantage point of the freedom of expression to be found in exile). Yet the very forms of expression permitted by not having to write with the fear of violent consequences led to some substantial differences. Moreover, the exiles' visibility as spokespersons on the conditions that had forced them to seek foreign refuge led inevitably to the assumption that their voices were coterminous with all of Argentine culture, and that they were speaking for all of the artists left behind whose voices had become silenced or distorted. In one sense, of course, they were. But the degree to which their freedom of expression allowed them to be eloquent spokespersons led to some resentment on the part of those who remained in Argentina and who felt that it was they who had the greatest witness to give about their nation. The fact that texts published in exile circulated widely and were frequently translated into prestige languages that enhanced their circulation only fueled this resentment. The debate as to who suffered most, those who remained behind to face the dreary horror of tyranny or those who experienced the wrenching dislocations of exile, is not seen to be spurious: human suffering cannot be calibrated in this way. But the fact remains that, beginning with Julio Cortázar, Manuel Puig, Luisa Valenzuela, and Osvaldo Soriano, it was often the writer in exile who led the way in defining what foreign reaction to Argentine culture under tyranny would be understood to consist of.

The third perspective is that of the foreign scholar, which may include Argentines who have become fully integrated in the American or European academic establishments. From the point of view of a foreign researcher, one is often struck by the lack of correspondence between what was going on in a nation like Argentina between 1976 and 1983 and the account of it that we have from abroad. This discrepancy resulted from both a lack of information and the distortions imposed by the military. While many have worked energetically to acquire a sense of what was happening in Argentina and what culture was being produced in response to it, the simple fact remains that a considerable amount of critical opinion has been produced on the basis of documents and texts published outside of Argentina as part of the aforementioned exile phenomenon. There is no reason to assume a tendentious harshness toward the academic community: Argentina is a long way away from most major academic centers, and the difficulties of assessing its social, cultural, and political life from abroad, assisted by regular research trips to the country, must necessarily be viewed as proceeding on the basis of honesty and good faith. But distortions do occur, beginning with the simple fact that foreign, chiefly American, observers enjoy a self-sufficient superiority that sometimes becomes all the more noticeable when they are most at pains to overcome it, and there is little that can be done to counter the feeling found in some quarters in Argentina that most of this scholarship produced in the United States or in Europe only touches the tip of the iceberg of all that has gone on in the nation.

The essays that are presented in this volume, several of which were written specifically to constitute a unified whole and several of which represent more than fifteen years of examining contestatorial phenomena as one category of Argentine literature, pretend both to set aside the disjunction between internal and external cultural production and to give credence to the possibility of writing coherently about a nation like Argentina from abroad. The best that I can say after twenty years of almost annual trips to Argentina, of one to two months in duration each year, is that I am confident both that the material represented here is one reasonable inventory of the literary culture produced in response to military tyranny, and that there is an abundant array of other texts that would justify a number of additional studies.

These essays place the greatest emphasis on narrative production, which should come as no surprise in view of the fact that Western societies continue to consume literature primarily in the form of the novel. Theater, however, is one of the greatest points of pride for Argentine (or, at least, Buenos Aires) society, and theater played an important role in challenging censorship, from which, as a public spectacle, it had suffered considerably. Sociopolitical commentary was, I argue, one of the innovative forms of expression during the early years of redemocratization, a genre both nurtured by the long tradition of professional journalism in Argentina (which also suffered authoritarian distortions and displayed numerous examples of self-serving cynicism) and stimulated by the need, after a decade of manipulated sources of information, of the people to "know the truth" and to seek it in allegedly less mediated forms of expression than the novel or the theater. The analyses of texts offered here will focus, in fact, on the strategies of mediation to be found in examples of sociopolitical commentary.

While the focus of these essays is on the period of military tyranny between 1976 and 1983 and on the period of redemocratization that immediately followed it, an important point must be made: the cultural production of a historical period does not refer solely to the works actually published during this period. Historians may be firmly tied to real dates. However, in forming an ideological analysis of the cultural production of a particular period, the way in which works are read is as much a part of their construction of meaning as the specific moment in which they are published. Thus, while Enrique Medina's *Las tumbas* (The tombs, 1972) was published prior to the period of the Proceso (in fact, during the junta governments between 1966 and 1973), it was reread, albeit clandestinely, during the Proceso, as a complex metaphor of the nation as a penal colony ruled by the hierarchical imposition of the law of the most brutal. Likewise, Alejandra Pizarnik's *La condesa sangrienta* (The Bloody Countess, 1971) was published in final book form during the military regime preceding the Proceso, one year before Pizarnik's suicide in 1972. However, it too became a clandestine classic, being reissued in 1976 and read, despite its immediate reference to a seventeenth-century Hungarian noblewoman, as an allegory of lawless, arbitrary power, shaded by the morbid fascination of the relationship between torture and sexual excitement. At the other end of the historic spectrum, a novel like Griselda Gambaro's *Lo impenetrable* (The impenetrable Madam X, 1984), while ostensibly a spoof of male-centered, pseudo-eighteenth-century pornography, also explores the restructuring of public morality made possible by the return to democracy: the decentering of male hegemony, represented paradigmatically by sober and brutal military institutions, in terms of female sexual initiative, with appropriate openings toward lesbian opportunities, is an emphatic recasting of the restrictive social culture authorized by a dictatorship driven by concerns other than those of individual rights. Thus, the period of military tyranny is a point of reference for cultural production, rather than a strictly chronological framework.[2]

Much else remains to be studied. I have examined elsewhere some examples of cartoon art,[3] and the study that a humor magazine such as *Humor registrado* (Copyrighted humor/Humor on record) deserves by virtue of its enormous subversive influence on public opinion has yet to be written. Now that the feverish film production of the first years of the Alfonsín government has petered out because of the unresolved economic situation, it is time to examine this body of cultural texts, many of which, like Luis Puenzo's *Historia oficial* (The Official Story, 1985), attracted enthusiastic international attention of the sort previously reserved only for Brazilian cinema and, in recent years, Spanish directors. Poetry, as always, seems to get ignored, although the highly private language of this genre may mean, in fact, that it was most able to escape censorship (including self-censorship) and, therefore, that it may upon examination reveal some of the most uncompromising writing of the period.[4]

A volume like this cannot escape the impression of being fragments of a mosaic whose boundaries are ill defined and outside its immediate scope. But this is in the nature of any society's production of culture: we have no reliable way of charting fixed boundaries, and any segment we choose to highlight is necessarily incomplete and, in a frustrating way, as much unrepresentative as it is representative. These essays, however, are presented as the reasonable typology of one foreign reader who has attempted, during twenty years of a cycle of military tyranny, to listen to the culture text generated in response to that tyranny.

2. For a study dealing more specifically with a historical circumscribed period, see Fernando Reati's excellent volume, *Nombrar lo innombrable* (To name the unnameable).

3. David William Foster, *From Mafalda to Los Supermachos: Latin American Graphic Humor as Popular Culture.*

4. For one published commentary to this effect, see Thorpe Running, "Responses to the Politics of Oppression by Poets in Argentina and Chile."

CHAPTER 1

Argentine Sociopolitical Commentary, the Malvinas Conflict, and Beyond

Rhetoricizing a National Experience

National culture is thus defined by the paralysis imposed by the fear of discovering ourselves, and as
long as this fear holds sway, the nation subjected to it
will continue to be identified much more with what
it hides than with what it shows of itself.

(La *cultura nacional* se define entonces por la parálisis
que impone el miedo a descubrirnos y, mientras im-
pere ese miedo, la nación a él sometida seguirá iden-
tificada mucho más con lo que oculta que con lo que
muestra de sí.)

—Santiago Kovadloff,
Una cultura de catacumbas (A culture of catacombs)

I

After the demise of the series of military dictatorships that
ruled Argentina so violently between 1976 and 1983, it was
inevitable that the return to democratic institutions would
bring with it an outpouring of the sorts of writing and cultural
activities banned and censored by the generals. Movie distributors
worked to meet the demand for the films that could not be seen

during these years (or that were only seen with extensive and capricious cuts). Theaters competed with each other to present works dealing with human rights violations and related themes. Television programming, which the military controlled assiduously, now began to reflect some social consciousness. And the print media filled bookstores and kiosks with myriad publications that bear witness to the attempt to recover a cultural tradition that was altered and fragmented by the so-called Proceso de Reorganización Nacional.

Yet as is often the case with attempts to control culture in a complex society, publications had already begun to circulate and the nonprint media had already begun to experiment with open expression before the elections in late 1983 that led to the inauguration of President Raúl Alfonsín, whose party, the Radicales, was committed to an open culture and a democratic society. Within Argentina, coverage of and response to the 1982 conflict with Great Britain over the Malvinas (Falkland Islands) provided an opening for considering how the ideology of the Proceso had led to this international conflict and what its relationship to life in Argentina had become. Furthermore, Argentine exiles who had lived through the early and most terrifying years of the Proceso and who had lost family and friends as a consequence of the military's *guerra sucia* (dirty war) published works abroad as part of the human rights campaign against the dictatorship. Some of these works were published in Spanish in Spain, while others appeared first in French or English.

Censorship in Argentina was officially abolished in November 1983 by the outgoing president, General Reynaldo Bignone. This act made possible the open and unrestricted circulation of new titles and the republication of writings by Argentine exiles that had been circulated only clandestinely before that date. It would be a simplification and a distortion of the history of culture in Argentina to say that no works of significant sociopolitical commentary were published within the country between 1976 and 1983. Many were, and many authors and their publishers suffered the consequences of defying a situation in which the rules were all too clear to everyone concerned. One need look no further than the fiction of Enrique Medina for an example of a writer who remained in Argentina and whose works constituted an open challenge to the official goal of a collective silence. *Las muecas del miedo* (The grimaces of fear, 1981) is perhaps the touchstone for this writing, and Medina was able to see his novel both escape censorship and sell widely. As its title would indicate, it deals with a national reality in which the grimaces of fear are the abiding constant.

But there is little question that beginning in late 1983 there has existed the possibility of the sort of free expression that disappeared in Argentina even before the military toppled the no less fascist regime of María Estela (a.k.a. Isabelita) Perón in March 1976 (it was during her government, from 1974 to 1976, that the AAA—La Alianza Anticomunista Argentina—began operations as a death squad to eliminate guerrillas and other subversives). In addition to an array of literary works, theatrical events, and artistic expositions, one finds an outpouring of sociopolitical commentary devoted to analyzing the country's recent experiences, both with the military regime and with the Malvinas war.

The goal of this study is to examine some of these writings— those that are most representative as a consequence of the prominence of their authors, the format of their text, and the specific aspects of Argentine social history with which they deal. My specific interest is not simply to summarize their subject matter or to synthesize the interpretations that they offer. Rather, I have chosen works that are particularly noteworthy, in my opinion, because of the discourse strategies employed in the development of the text. We have come to accept contemporary theories of cultural writing in which it is argued that no text can be simply the innocently transparent exposition of meaning, but that all writing is instead an ideologically conditioned rhetoricizing of the reality it purports to represent. It is therefore natural to approach documents dealing with intense social conflicts such as one finds in the contemporary Argentine national experience from the point of view of the writer's inescapable need to elaborate a rhetorically persuasive discourse. In this sense, the works I have chosen to analyze are not just those in which the rhetorical superstructure is most immediately evident or impressive. Instead, the works examined in the following pages are those that I consider to be most interesting because of the coherence of the rhetorical strategies employed.

This study seeks to address the ways in which the authors view their activities as sociopolitical commentary. It deduces for examination the authors' presuppositions about their implied readers, the manner in which they bracket events of recent Argentine history, and the structural patterns that they suggest give meanings to these events. Attention will be paid to the rhetorical strategies employed in the attempt to elaborate a text that proposes to explain these events and their meaning. Of particular interest will be how the author or narrator mediates in the text as a voice or character and the degree to which narrativization—the representation in terms of a cause-and-effect sequence of events portrayed through "characters" (historical or otherwise)—is a primary textual strategy in these writings. All writing is, in some sense, rhetoric; I am not asserting that these texts have some privileged claim to persuasive efficacy. What is especially interesting is to observe the development of a rhetoric capable of speaking on certain still painful issues. If the reader is drawn to the works primarily because of their content, it is their individual rhetoric that makes them interesting as cultural documents at a particular juncture in Argentine history.

II

Lastly, I express my gratitude to the article of the Constitution of my country, which supported the publication of this work.

(Por último, expreso mi gratitud a los artículos de la Constitución de mi país que amparan la edición de esta obra.)

—Marcos Aguinis,
Carta esperanzada a un general: puente cobre el abismo

Marcos Aguinis (1935) is a medical doctor who has received considerable attention for his fiction; his novel *La cruz invertida* (The inverted cross, 1970) is perhaps his best-known work. Although he is a major spokesman for a liberal and critical segment of the Argentine Jewish community, his fictional writings as a whole probe the spiritual malaise, emotional uneasiness, and psychological disorientation of successful middle-class Argentines. The ways in which his characters address the simple fact that they are not happy with how they live their lives constitute one literary image of the forces at work beneath the bourgeois gentility and urban comfort of Argentina today.

With *Carta esperanzada a un general: puente sobre el abismo* (Hopeful letter to a general: Bridge over the abyss, 1983), Aguinis addresses some of the issues confronting contemporary Argentine society, using an essayistic format as an alternative to the forms of fictional narration characteristic of his novels and short stories. Although the essay was published in December 1983, when it was clear that a transition to democracy would take place, *Hopeful Letter* is dated "June–July 1983"—that is, before elections were held in Argentina and before Alfonsín was sworn in as president. Nevertheless, Aguinis obviously prepared his letter with the clear conviction that elections would be held (he campaigned for Alfonsín and served as an undersecretary and the secretary of culture in the Radical administration), in the firm belief that a transition to democracy would take place, and with the hope that it would once again be possible to hold an open and frank dialogue on national issues, such as is guaranteed by the Argentine constitution. The entire text of *Hopeful Letter* is predicated on these assumptions, which are necessary presuppositions for its meaning as distinguishing characteristics of either the present status of free speech in Argentina or its future as the Alfonsín government addresses the complex forces that shape Argentina's political life.

As a statement of ideas definable in sociopolitical terms, *Hopeful Letter* is a meticulous and unyielding dissection of the sort of military mentality that has made such a mockery out of Argentina's claim to participate in the orbit of American- and European-style liberal democratic traditions. The fact that the military has repeat-edly violated the constitution under the guise of defending it is but one thread in the argument Aguinis pursues. As an example of an essay structured along the lines of identifiable rhetorical strategies, *Hopeful Letter* makes use of the conventional epistolary format whereby the role of the addressee in an idealized dialogue is usurped by a gracious but unrelenting speaker.

Aguinis's fundamental point of departure is the notion of lan-guage (as the verbal articulation of ideas), speech (as a pragmatic act of information exchange through language), and communica-tion (as a successful intellectual and spiritual exchange). The title of his essay makes explicit reference to one of the oldest tropes to describe the nature of dialogue: it is a bridge spanning an abyss. In this case, the abyss is a consequence of the entire network of ideas and values that separates the military from the civilian mind and experience and that gives rise to the idea of a problem of communication between the military and civilians. Thus *Hopeful Letter*, addressed to a prototypic General and signed by one Mar-cos Aguinis, will constitute a text that undertakes to bridge this abyss. The act of writing in *Hopeful Letter* is a material gesture of communication subordinate to the dominant trope of the essay, whereby language and speech are the "bridge" and communica-tion overcomes the abyss that alludes to the distance between the Argentine people and one of its prime social institutions.

Clearly, the fictional image of a letter confirms the importance of the allusions to language and communication, either as a pri-vate correspondence to which we happen to have access or as an open document in which a larger public beyond the specifically addressed audience is implicated. In the first place, Aguinis charac-terizes military formation (that is, officer training), which he prefers to pun as "de-formation," as built on the deforming deprivation of language and communication; deprived of language, the individ-ual is deprived of identity.[1] *Hopeful Letter* functions by asserting,

---

1. Marcos Aguinis, *Carta esperanzada a un general: puente sobre el abismo*, 18–19, hereafter cited parenthetically in the text.

if only by implication, that this situation of deprivation and its deforming consequences can be critically dealt with in a document such as the one addressed to the General and which we, as readers, are privileged to examine. Thus Aguinis, with considerable irony for the presumed benefit of his readers, addresses the General as unique in his willingness to read the letter, to consider the issues it raises, and then to persevere in the face of assertions that are necessarily unsettling if not scandalous for the institution the General represents. Expressions of the writer's gratitude to the General for continuing to read the text are complemented by observations as to how unique his addressee must indeed be, given the need of the military mind to avert unreflexively its gaze from—in a word, to censor—any expression of criticism toward it from outside its own ranks.

Aguinis's text thus proceeds as though there is a possibility of communication, even though that possibility is repeatedly questioned and denied by his own analyses of the military's aversion toward open dialogue and communication uncircumscribed by institutional deformation. This characterization is heightened by Aguinis's use of pathological metaphors like "enfermedad autoritaria" (authoritarian illness).[2]

A corollary of the epistolary fiction of *Hopeful Letter* is this disjunctive characterization of a military dysfunctional language versus the free exchange of communication characteristic of the democracy the military regime inevitably opposes and represses. For what makes Aguinis's text an example of free speech is, in addition to the overtly articulated sociopolitical theses it contains, the possibility for communication it exemplifies. That it is addressed to a General who must read the text through (if he were to abandon its reading or to destroy it, there would be no text for the circumstantial reader to glimpse) is an expression of faith in the possibility for a healthy dynamic of communication to be (re)established in a nation where so many events have conspired against it.

---

2. In "Hacia una tipología del discurso autoritario," Beatriz R. Lavandera provides a fascinating discourse analysis of the structure of authoritarianism.

It is for this reason that the epistolary format used by Aguinis is so rhetorically conceitful. *Hopeful Letter* is ostensibly addressed to an unnamed General, but it is, of course, read in practice by the purchasers of the book, those interested in Aguinis's writing, those attracted to the topic, chance readers, or whomever. I do not call the letter artifice of the text a fiction because Aguinis is uninterested in his comments being read by the Argentine generals; the sort of communication Aguinis sought was necessary at a time when Argentina was returning to democracy and the demand was being made that the military redefine its role in national life, especially within the context of the 1984 trials convened, with great public support, against members and subordinates.

However, the artifice of the text comes from the fact of its publication as a book, and as a consequence the epistolary format is but the basic structural principal underlying the published text. The implications of this circumstance are evident. In the first place, there is a disjunction between the overt addressee of the text and actual readers. If the General—"the generals," as the common synecdoche for the military in Latin America goes—is both the intended reader (the one that is explicitly identified) and the ideal reader (a certain sort of General who will agree to follow Aguinis in his exposition, no matter how offensive it may be to conventional military self-images), the "real" or "actual" readers of the text must necessarily be the broad spectrum of Argentines who read Aguinis, who buy books, and who are interested in cultural and sociopolitical topics like the one broached by *Hopeful Letter*. Thus, the ostensible reader, a potentially hostile General but one who the author hopes is curious enough to read the document, is necessarily supplemented by actual readers who in varying degrees are sympathetic to Aguinis's point of view and his discursive strategies.

The supplemental nature of the civilian readers of *Hopeful Letter* is reflected in the essential tone of the text. The conventional polite formulas of epistolary address are complemented by numerous ironic, perhaps even sarcastic, asides. The unrelentingly trenchant characterization of military (de)formation undermines the formal graciousness of the epistolary format. Meticulous demonstrations

of the internal contradictions of the military point of view com-
plement insistent dissections of the commonplaces—titles, formulas, slogans, bywords—of military life in a fashion that would be
considered boorish in a real-life dialogue, whether face-to-face or
epistolary.

The result is that, despite the apostrophes to the General that
open each of the thirty-two excursi into which *Hopeful Letter* is
divided and the various other direct appeals to him throughout
the text, Aguinis's essay quickly defines a secondary ideal reader,
one who is not explicitly identified but who accepts the fundamental legitimacy of the author's line of inquiry. If congratulating
the General for his willingness to persevere in reading *Hopeful
Letter* is a necessary rhetorical disingenuousness, *Hopeful Letter*
is sincere in its assumption that there are legions of Argentine
readers who do not need to be convinced of the legitimacy of
its sociopolitical presuppositions. This is particularly true in the
many passages in which the author attacks the military worldview.
Italics, quotation marks, rhetorical questions, and expressions of
exclamation all serve to characterize the author's assumptions. The
latter may be diametrically opposed to those of the overt addressee
of *Hopeful Letter*, but they are intended to be recognized as valid
formulations of the real readers of the text. Hence, direct references
to the General become in effect a gesture behind his back to the
real readers.

Hopeful Letter thus becomes essentially a text of attribution, demanding that both the explicit addressee and the nonovert secondary addressee accept the characterization of the military worldview. The unrelenting presentation of contradictions, ill-founded
assumptions, vacuous clichés, unresolvable oppositions, antilogies,
and the like provides for a text that Aguinis's real readers will be
likely to endorse after witnessing recent Argentine history. The
defining characteristic of *Hopeful Letter* is the irony that its explicit
addressee is not likely to accept the legitimacy of this characterization of the military mind and, moreover, of the right to criticize it
from a civilian point of view, no matter how gracious and hopeful
a tone the author assumes. It is the disjunction between this fact

and the therapeutic image of communication on which *Hopeful Letter* is based that defines the special features as discourse in Aguinis's essay.

One final point: Aguinis cannot lose, so to speak, in the strategic discursive gamble represented by his letter. In the first place, the fact that it is a "private" letter made public by the act of publication implies an inescapable acknowledgment of its existence on the part of the paradigmatic addressee: overt acknowledgment of its existence brings with it by implication a measure of willingness to at least engage in the exchange of ideas proposed by a dialogue between two persons and, therefore, by encouraging the General to contemplate himself in the mirror of the author's text, the possibility that the addressee may be right in his opinions. The failure to acknowledge the existence of the letter can only serve to confirm one of the major hypotheses of Aguinis's statements: that the military mind is incapable of entertaining differences of opinion. To be sure, these possibilities occur offstage, outside the actual enunciation of the text. However, from the point of view of the participation of *Hopeful Letter* in the Argentine sociopolitical text, this interchange is one of the inevitable consequences of Aguinis's epistolary strategy.

III

Two recurring motifs in the sociopolitical writings have appeared in Argentina since the Malvinas conflict and the return to constitutional democracy. On the one hand, there is the imperative to reveal a secret or hidden reality—the circumstances of the plans for social, economic, and political control by a series of dictatorial military governments, of which the Argentine people possessed only the sketchiest notion while those governments were in power. The people suffered daily the effects of this control. But because of censorship and the denial of free access to information, they had only a fragmentary perception of the extent of the operations undertaken in the name of the Proceso. These writings undertake to set forth the full details as they have become known.

The second goal is a logical extension of the first one. It is not enough to inform the Argentine people that a well-wrought program of institutionalized terror was an integral part of the Proceso. Readers must be convinced that the horrifying story being outlined for them is indeed accurate, that it is not a yellow journalism exaggeration of the facts but that considerable corroborative documentary evidence exists. Eduardo Luis Duhalde's *El estado terrorista argentino* (The Argentine terrorist state, 1983), like Cardoso, Kirschbaum, and van der Kooy's *Las Malvinas: la trama secreta* (Falklands: The secret plot, 1983, see discussion later in this chapter), is in the best tradition of contemporary investigative reporting. (Duhalde served as vice president of Argentina from 1989 to 1991; in 1991 he was elected governor of the Province of Buenos Aires.) Little pretense is made to dramatize the information for greater effect, although many verbatim reports from victims and witnesses are quoted in point-by-point fashion. Duhalde is a lawyer, journalist, and university professor who worked, after leaving Argentina in late 1976, with the Comisión Argentina de Derechos Humanos (Argentine Human Rights Commission), which provided him with the opportunity to assemble the documentary information and to interview the individuals quoted in *The Argentine Terrorist State*. His exposition follows a meticulous outline, and the book's three parts deal in turn with the establishment of the terrorist state (the March 1976 coup and its goals); the mechanics of the regime of terror (the pattern of arrest, torture, prison, and death synthesized by reference to the victim as a *desaparecido* [disappeared]); and a description of the struggle against the regime. Like many of the books dealing with recent Argentine history, *The Argentine Terrorist State* was first published abroad (in Spain); an Argentine edition was published following the return to democracy.

Duhalde constructs his documentary presentation on the premise that the military government that came to power in 1976 legitimized itself by exploiting the article of the Argentine constitution permitting a "state of exception" in the event of a threat to national security. The unilateral definition of such a threat and the military coup in response to it allowed the military to dissolve the already tottering government of María Estela de Perón and to implement the Proceso, which Duhalde argues had as its basic goal to maintain Argentina's dependent place in a capitalistic order at the expense of popular demands for social and economic reforms. Thus, the title of his book is an oxymoron that defines his interpretation of the military's response to political circumstances in Argentina in the mid–1970s. If the notion of "state" refers to a constitutional order, the terrorist state that came into existence in Argentina in 1976 involved a program of institutionalized violence that contradicts the entire notion of constitutional guarantees and legal due process. A logical extension of this corrupt use of the text of the constitution to create a terrorist state is the need to create a paralegal reality. If on the surface of everyday public life the government preaches the patriotic goals of its process of national reconstruction and moral realignment, it pursues clandestinely a program for the silencing and elimination of any vestige of opposition. This alternate, secret reality—which Duhalde and the other writers of this study are concerned with revealing in detail—is the antiphonic text to the public declarations of the military government:

> *Physically annihilate the enemy* was the order given on March 26, 1976. Kill, assassinate, execute, but with the characteristics of *clandestinity and simulation* that we have narrated throughout this work.
> "I allege publicly that in Argentina during a long period no one wanted to recognize that the country was at war, this to protect its image abroad, and so as not to compromise international economic assistance the truth of the facts was not spoken. There was a desire to downplay reality in order to maintain the credits, which without a doubt would have been suspended if the truth in all of its cruelty were articulated."
> The pretorian General [Ramón] Camps does not hesitate to recognize the existence of clandestine and simulated actions. He also explains one of the justifying reasons for the refusal to recognize what was being mounted daily by the repressive apparatus of the

State. Of course, he does not explain *the forms in which the policy of assassination was covered up.*)

(*Aniquilar físicamente al enemigo*, fue la orden del 24 de marzo de 1976. Matar, asesinar, ejecutar, pero con las características de *clandestinidad y simulación* que hemos narrado a lo largo de este trabajo.

"Yo sostengo públicamente que en la Argentina durante un largo período, no se quiso reconocer que el país vivía en guerra, en aras de la imagen exterior y para no comprometer las ayudas económicas internacionales, no se decía la verdad de los hechos. Se quería minimizar la realidad, pensando en la continuidad de los créditos, que seguramente tampoco se habrían interrumpido si se hubiese planteado la verdad en toda su crueldad."

El pretoriano General [Ramón] Camps, no vacila en reconocer la existencia del accionar clandestino y simulado. También explica una de las razones justificantes de la negativa a reconocer lo que se instrumentaba cotidianamente desde el aparato represivo del Estado. No explica, claro está, *las formas de ocultamiento de la política de asesinatos.*)[3]

While the general outlines of Duhalde's book follow the clear plan of contemporary journalistic reporting, the contrast between the public voice of the junta and the clandestine actions for the elimination of dissent and opposition provides the essential rhetorical strategy of his exposition. The contextualization of the military's hidden activities involves a series of redefinitions that begin with the structural features of government and extend to Argentina's complex cultural institutions. Duhalde's approach is to show not only that events were far worse than they appeared to be (the people stopped on the street or taken from their homes by armed agents were not being arrested by policemen discharging their legal function) but also that the events the public was able to witness and on which the heavily censored press was able to report were only

3. Duhalde, *El estado terrorista argentino*, 221, hereafter cited parenthetically in the text. See Ramón J. A. Camps, *Caso Timerman: punto final*, for a version of the dirty war from the perspective of the chief of police operations in Buenos Aires.

the prelude to a horrible, clandestine drama (those people entered an underworld of torture, imprisonment, and extermination). The details of Duhalde's book present a new social reality both far more complex and far more nefarious than that of simply another in a long line of repressive military governments.

Of particular prominence is the analysis of the duplicitous nature of the government's language. In addition to the false texts of the junta's self-legitimizing documents, the public language of government undergoes a transformation whereby, because of the need to ignore and deny a clandestine reality that is impinging daily on the lives of more and more citizens, words are used euphemistically and cynically to convey meanings that bespeak the new social reality (138; see also 159 on the language of the interrogators and 221–23 on the vocabulary of the processes of extermination).

Duhalde's book may lack the sustained narrativization characteristic of most of the documents examined in this study. With the exception of the personal narratives of the witnesses whose testimonies are included as documentary corroboration, *The Argentine Terrorist State* is more strictly journalistic. Yet the burden of reconstructing and interpreting an intricate social reality ("writing about the terrorist state, when the latter is based on the suffering and blood of our brethren is a task that is neither easy nor agreeable" [escribir sobre el Estado Terrorista, cuando éste se asienta sobre el dolor y la sangre de nuestros hermanos, no es tarea fácil ni agradable, 10]) leads inevitably to a set of rhetorical strategies that provides the book with a great measure of its coherence.

IV

Carlos Gabetta's *Todos somos subversivos* (We are all subversive, 1983) must count as one of the core documents in the analysis of contemporary sociopolitical writing in Argentina. Although the Argentine Spanish language edition only became possible with the return to democracy, a French language edition had appeared four years earlier as part of the considerable effort made by Argentine exiles and their supporters to influence international opinion against the military regime.

Read in French, *We Are All Subversive* is an eloquent series of personal testimonials by individuals who were the victims of the dirty war or, as the propaganda of the dictatorship later preferred to put it when it grew clear that they were no longer "merely" killing guerrillas but were persecuting citizens innocent of any violation of the criminal code, the Proceso de Reorganización Nacional. These victims were the parents and loved ones of the disappeared, individuals who themselves had suffered arbitrary arrest, torture, and incarceration, and people who were living in exile in France and other parts of the world as a consequence of exercising their constitutionally guaranteed rights. On the other hand, read in the delayed Argentine edition, *We Are All Subversive* is no longer simply the casebook record, a relentless chronicle of human suffering. It is the formulation of the response to the lies of those guilty of the repression of the Argentine citizenry that could not, until the formal return of democracy in late 1983, be articulated in Argentina. In a very real sense, the publication of Gabetta's interviews in the original Argentine Spanish in which they were conducted is not simply the supplanting of the French translation by the Spanish original: it is the restoration of the original voice of the individuals interviewed, and it is in this sense that it is a significant cultural document.

Gabetta conducted the interviews for *We Are All Subversive* around 1979. In Argentina, Gabetta was a journalist specializing in political affairs, working both in radio and with newspapers and magazines; he also wrote several books dealing with sociopolitical issues. Like several hundred of his fellow journalists, Gabetta was in exile at the time he conducted the interviews. But in writing *We Are All Subversive*, Gabetta was in a position unlike that of most journalists. Rather than playing the customary journalistic role of a detached observer or objective professional who in a certain sense is a voyeur of the unusual and noteworthy experiences of the interviewee, Gabetta shared the experience of exile with the persons whose testimony he sought out. This means that he too is one of the *we* of the title. In answering Gabetta's questions and in responding to his request that they tell their story, his interviewees are also telling Gabetta's own story.

The slippage between an objective journalistic distance and the reporter's personal involvement in what he is reporting is at the heart of the discourse structure of *We Are All Subversive*. The principal thrust of Gabetta's interviews emerges very straightforwardly in an ironically syllogistic fashion: The military identified as subversive all those who, in their exercise of constitutionally guaranteed rights, protested its arbitrary rule and violent repression; all Argentines shared to one degree or another in the devastation and suffering imposed by the military regime in the pursuit of its self-assigned and self-serving programs; therefore, all Argentines are subversive. Of course, the terrible truth of this syllogism is borne out by the fact that so many Argentines from all walks of life and political persuasions were affected directly or indirectly by the repression of the Proceso, and the range of the people that Gabetta interviews is unquestionably meant to bear witness to this avowed fact.

Beginning with the premise that all Argentines are subversive in the meaning imposed by the military has a number of rhetorical consequences for the texts of Gabetta's interviews and our understanding of them. In the first place, the word *subversivo* becomes a trope, in the sense of a term that is used in distorted or twisted fashion. Gabetta's text—the text of his questions, of his interviewee's responses, and of his own intercalated observations—begins with the premise that the military regime used the word in a deliberately misleading fashion. While it is true that there were those individuals committed to guerrilla activity and to revolutionary overthrow of the military regime, Gabetta is concerned not with these individuals (whom the military had effectively neutralized within a year or so of its ascension to power), but with ordinary citizens labeled as subversive because of their various forms of legal opposition to the regime; and, of course, one might also note that there were those who were identified as subversive as the result of private vendettas or as the consequence of guilt by association.

Thus, Gabetta's title is in reality a trope of a trope: it is the deliberately distorted use of a term on the basis of a prior deliberate distortion of it. One of the key segments of the book concerns Senator Hipólito Solari Yrigoyen. Solari Yrigoyen, the grandnephew of Hipólito Yrigoyen, Argentina's first populist president who was overthrown during his second term in office by Argentina's first military coup in September 1930, had a long record of opposition to the military regime. It was only because of international pressure and the agency of the Venezuelan government that Solari Yrigoyen was able to leave the country alive: many lawyers, politicians, and public men who acted legally in the commonweal were tortured and murdered as a matter of routine. Solari Yrigoyen speaks in detail of the charges the military made against him.[4] During his recitation of these charges and their consequences for both his personal experiences of persecution and the cynical corruption of meaning imposed by the "military mentality," Gabetta intercalates his contrapuntal interior monologue:

> But Hipólito, you are a lost cause as a subversive! One of those delinquents who deserve to be on display with Pibe Cabezas, Scarface, and the Baader Gang . . . Who, except for an agent of international communism, a man without a country, an atheist collectivist, would think to denounce the repression in the Parliament, oppose the coverups of the union bureaucracy, doubt the good faith of our heroic navy, army, and air force in their handling of the affairs of the country, and, to top it all off, publish books!
>
> (Pero Hipólito, ¡usted es un subversivo irrecuperable! Un delincuente de ésos que merecería estar en la galería junto al Pibe Cabeza, Scarface y la Banda Baader . . . ¿A quién, sino a un agente del comunismo internacional, a un apátrida, a un colectivista ateo, se le ocurriría denunciar la represión en el Parlamento, oponerse a los enjuagues de la burocracia sindical, sospechar de la buena fe de nuestros heróicos marinos, infantes y aviadores en el manejo de los negocios del país y, encima, publicar libros!) (246)

4. Gabetta, *Todos somos subversivos*, 226, hereafter cited parenthetically in the text.

Gabetta's sarcasm here is simply one emphatic example of the recurring theme in *We Are All Subversive* that the military dictatorship, in order to justify its unchecked reign of terror, defined subversion in such a way that it could be applied effortlessly to any citizen with a shred of belief in Argentina's much abused constitution. Since the agents of subversion have been military officers who have led coups against constitutionally elected presidents, what they customarily mean by subversion is what is both legal and constitutional. Therefore, Argentines must accept with pride the accusation that they are all subversive. This line of thinking is saved from being simply rhetorically ingenious by the ample references to unknowing collaboration by the military in the postulation of Gabetta's guiding conceit.

Concomitant with using the term *subversive* as a trope is the image of Gabetta's interviews as the appropriate response to the years of official lies propagated with all of the advantage held by dictatorships. Troping the military's trope means also refuting the barrage of propaganda with the simple truth of his interviewee's testimonials. Of course, the reader has no way to verify that what these people say is the truth, and their stories must be accepted in an act of goodwill by readers who accept the premise of the repressive nature of the military dictatorships in Argentina. But it is not important, from the point of view of discourse strategies, for us to be able to verify or validate the testimonials of the interviewees. It is sufficient for us to believe them to be true in substance for the rhetoric of *We Are All Subversive* to function, though we might also be able to verify the details satisfactorily.

Another variation of the same calculus of interrelationship between truth and propaganda is the utterance of a denied truth, the recovery of the possibility to affirm a truth that repression, by the very nature of its root meaning, had made it impossible to express (165–66). Thus, the unifying motif of Gabetta's interviews is the opportunity to speak about these sufferings, to tell one's own story and at the same time to articulate a version of a national, collective experience that, from the perspective of official propaganda, is nothing but a subversive lie. As a previously silenced sociopolitical history, the texts gathered together in *We Are All Subversive* in the mosaic fashion typical of contemporary narratives propose both to undermine official lies and to remedy the generalized sense of an unstable and unclear collective identity that results from cynical propaganda.

In conformance with this motif, Gabetta's interviews, whether natural, spontaneous conversations or a carefully crafted discourse that strives for the impression of such conversations, are a network of allusions to sociopolitical events in Argentina since the Onganía coup in June 1966 and to intertextual echoes of the disingenuous propaganda of the entire machinery of repression. All of this contributes to an image of documentary authenticity, by virtue of the fact that *We Are All Subversive* implies a reader who accepts implicitly the legitimacy of the postulates and assumptions on which it is based, which is ultimately more significant than whether or not the specific interviews are verifiably factual or accurate in every detail. Thus, should subsequent journalistic writings contradict the points covered by the long interview with Senator Solari Yrigoyen or repudiate the details of incarceration provided by the exiles, there would be no significant alteration in the fundamental structure of Gabetta's narrative.

V

At times reality becomes strange. . . .

The passions of six, ten years ago have turned into photographs on my desk. All of Argentina fits into a pile of yellow file folders which I consult out of exasperation. Far away and long ago is no longer Hudson's cheery title which, because it was so felicitous, became a commonplace. It is an obsession that visits my thoughts day and night, at any time of the day. . . .

I think about what the photograph shows and also what it hides. And I know that I will either lack words or have too many to express it.

a veces la realidad se pone rara [. . .].
Las pasiones de hace seis, diez años atrás, se han
convertido en fotografías sobre el escritorio. La Argentina entera cabe en una montonera de carpetas
amarillas, que consulto con exasperación. Allá lejos y
hace tiempo no es más el título feliz de Hudson que,
de tan feliz, devino lugar común. Es una obsesión que
visita al pensamiento día y noche, a cada hora. [. . .]
Pienso en lo que la foto muestra y también en lo que
oculta. Y sé que me van a faltar o me van a sobrar
palabras para expresarlo.

—Miguel Bonasso,
Recuerdo de la muerte

Miguel Bonasso's *Recuerdo de la muerte* (Souvenir of death, 1984)
has two features that set it off from other works examined in this
study. In the first place, its image of the military repression in
Argentina between 1976 and 1983 refers exclusively to the struggle between the armed forces and the Montoneros, the left-wing
guerrilla segment of the multifaceted Peronista party. The Montoneros saw themselves as embodying the true spirit of social rev-
olution of the original Peronista program, which had been ignored
by self-serving party hacks who controlled official Peronismo in
the wake of Evita's death and Perón's ill health and subsequent
death after his triumphant return to Argentina in 1973. Perón's
third wife, María Estela Martínez, who succeeded him as president
in 1974, and her adviser, the nefarious José López Rega, were
accused of initiating the "fascistic" repression that the military
continued and expanded after their takeover in 1976. Ostracized
by the segments of the party in power virtually since Perón's
return and persecuted relentlessly by the military after 1976, the
Montoneros saw themselves as the true but persecuted nucleus of
La Argentina Peronista.[5] Bonasso, who served as press secretary

---

5. Juan José Sebreli, *Los deseos imaginarios del peronismo.*

for the outlawed Montoneros at their exile headquarters in Mexico City, has chosen to write of the prison experiences in Argentina of Montonero personalities and of the activities in exile of their commanders, who sought both to save them from death and to publicize their continued presence in Argentina for the cause of the Montonero movement.

The result is an undeniably intriguing story. For any reader who has not maintained one of the yellow file folders *(carpetas amarillas)* Bonasso speaks of, the presumedly historically identifiable individuals who move through the narrative take on the qualities of fictional characters in a novelized chronicle. This is the second distinguishing characteristic of Bonasso's book: his decision to provide an account that is as novelistic as possible. It is this quality of *Souvenir of Death* as novel that is both its principal characteristic and its principal rhetorical problem.

Any account is a narrative if it is based on a series of actions that follow a cause-and-effect pattern. Narratives are only fictional if there is some appeal to the reader (such as by appending, after the title, the epithet "novel") to suspend the journalist's or the historian's imperative that the facts portrayed be susceptible to verification. Readers are accustomed to believing that there is a clear-cut break between history and fiction, and that narrative accounts belong expressly to one category or the other. However, just as some forms of historical narration may make use of literary devices in order to highlight and enhance the image of human experience they relate, the contemporary novel has often explored the rhetorical possibilities of documentary fiction, the nonfiction novel, new journalism, and the like.[6] The result is the blurring of the distinction between history and novel (and a cataloger's headache), as well as a suspension of the question of whether the historian or the novelist provides the most valuable account of human affairs. Of course, one might also note that there is a major epistemological distinction to be made between documentary nar-

6. David William Foster, "Latin American Documentary Narrative."

ratives and fiction, since only the latter can verisimilarly allow the dead and the disappeared to speak on their own.

Souvenir of Death, although it covers a lot of ground in surveying the military persecution of the Montoneros (so many people are mentioned that an index would be useful), deals primarily with the story of Jaime Dri. Dri, whose father was a Peronista leader in the province of El Chaco, served as a Diputado in the 1973–1976 Peronista government; as a member of the Montoneros he was an important figure in the high command in the industrial port city of Rosario. During an operation for the Montoneros in Uruguay in late 1977, Dri is captured in Uruguay and returned to Argentina. He is eventually sequestered in the Navy's Escuela de Mecánica close to downtown Buenos Aires, one of the most infamous of the torture centers and concentration camps. (Because of its proximity to one of the stadiums used for the 1978 World Soccer Cup Matches held in Argentina, human rights groups and the international press made it a symbol of military repression in Argentina.)[7]

During his imprisonment, Dri moves in a Dantean inferno of physical torture, mental anguish, and terrible death. He discovers what in retrospect is one of the most ludicrous aspects of the entire Proceso during the dark years of the late 1970s. Despite the public image of a united military front against the "enemigos de la Patria," there was in fact much of the usual sort of interagency military rivalry. In Argentina, this has been particularly the case between the army, which traditionally dominated the juntas, and the navy, which tended to view itself as the more aristocratic service.

The story is a complicated one, but its general outlines, as discovered by Dri and reported by Bonasso, are as follows: Emilio Eduardo Massera, the navy's commander, nurtured presidential ambitions. Seeing himself as a possible successor to the charis-

7. For an interesting analysis of the ideologization of soccer in 1978 by the military junta, see Neil Larsen, "Sport as Civil Society: The Argentine Junta Plays Championship Soccer." Douglas Mine's novel, *Champions of the World* (1988), is an interesting fictional account of the 1978 matches and their sociopolitical dimensions in Argentina. Mine's novel is discussed in my "Imagining Argentine Socio-Political History."

matic Perón in achieving a national unity, Massera felt that rather than slaughtering the "subversives" wholesale, they should be captured and co-opted. The Escuela de Mecánica was the place used for this risky undertaking, which the army command thoroughly disapproved of (indeed, there was serious competition between the two branches for the same prisoners). Individuals who had been arrested and persuaded to become turncoats for one reason or another (to save themselves from torture and death, to protect family members, to take advantage of new possibilities for power) fingered comrades, aided in the navy's intelligence operations, and in general subverted what remained of the Montoneros' organization in Argentina and abroad. Bonasso calls them at one point "Preachers of Repentence" (Predicadores del Arrepentimiento), since Massera claimed to believe that, once they had repented of their antisocial ways, they would convince other comrades to do the same.

While pretending to go along with this arrangement, Dri plans a successful escape at the time of the Copa Mundial in mid–1978. Bonasso's book is the account of Dri's experiences. In the course of reconstructing them for the reader, Bonasso is able to survey the activities of the Montoneros during the period since Perón's death, to describe for the reader the outlines of Massera's fantastic project (surely it is a project that, as the plot of a novel, would be thoroughly unbelievable), and to describe for the reader the sickening details of the apparatus of repression mounted by the military in its goal to reaffirm Argentina as a "Christian and Western" society. Bonasso strives for a well-paced narrative, and in the process he avails himself of all of the features associated with the novel: stream of consciousness, interior monologue, ironic juxtaposition of narrative segments, fragmentation of time and space, strategic intrusions by an omniscient narrator, flashbacks, and so on. The result combines features of the conventional spy novel and the contemporary postmodernist novel. To all of this is added the element of the reader's morbid fascination with the revelation of a monstrous secret world. The following passage is an example of Bonasso's narrative strategies in this regard. El Tigre, one of the authorities at the Escuela, is attempting to seduce Pelusa with the promise of freeing her family, also held in prison. Although he has personally tortured her and is free to rape her at any time, his self-image demands that he court her in a conventional fashion. One night he takes her out from prison on a date to an elegant restaurant and courts her as though she were a highly prized woman of class, even to the extent of buying flowers for her from the prototypical little old lady vendor (285–86). One might be tempted to dismiss this sort of writing as a Third World imitation of cheap paperbacks purporting to detail romances in Nazi concentration camps, leavened with purple-prose evocations of "zo my pretty maiden" abuse. However, Bonasso's story, by detailing events and referring to individuals who can be historically verified, demands that the reader accept it as unequivocally true. The fact that the recent history of Argentina has tended to outstrip the imagination of even the most vigorous fabulator makes it difficult to accept the narrator's assertions as anything other than substantially true. As a consequence of the urgency of Argentine readers' need to know the facts of the events between 1976 and 1983, Bonasso is able to count on a high degree of suspension of disbelief for his narrative.

Yet the narrative features that give *Souvenir of Death* so much novelistic coloring also make it difficult to analyze the work's internal coherence. Unlike the other documents I have examined, which appeal to the reader either as varieties of historical research (Aguinis, Cardoso, and others), journalistic inquiry (Kon, Cardoso, and others), or as forthright chronicles of facts gathered by the author (Duhalde), Bonasso's book raises serious questions about the source of his information and the strategies of presentation. Let us leave aside the question of whether or not the facts Bonasso reports are accurate, objective, and neutral; it is necessary for a historian to judge them in this regard. What I am referring to are the materials that Bonasso accumulated in his yellow file folders on the basis of the usual activities of a reporter—interviews with individuals at the time of events and subsequent to them and parallel research among documents. Certainly, Bonasso would have interviewed Dri and many of the other persons mentioned in *Souvenir of Death*, and there is no question that an elaborate chronicle could have been constructed from such sources. However, Bonasso is not satisfied merely to reconstruct the outlines of events and to report what people said to him, evaluating in the process his personal views on what they told him. Rather, in enhancing the narrativity of his book, he chooses to supplement the documentarily and journalistically verifiable with an entire range of psychological perspectives that are typical of the repertory of the writer of fiction. Let us admit the possibility that Dri and his companions could share with Bonasso their interior monologues and streams of consciousness during the various stages of their capture, torture, and imprisonment. Even though these passages might be more re-creations than recollections, attribution to the individuals themselves may provide a comfortable measure of confirmation that does not belie Bonasso's implied goal of historical accuracy.

However, a serious problem arises when dealing with parties to whom Bonasso could not have had direct access. In addition to the dead, this would include the agents of military repression and high government officials. Yet the narrator homologizes their presentation to that of persons like Dri, with whom we will have had direct contact. Both in the form of interior monologues and stream of consciousness and in the use of free indirect discourse ("X thought such and such," "Y imagined this and that"), they figure as characters in the narrative to as full an extent as Dri and his companions. This is most notable in the case of Dri's antagonist, the navy man nicknamed El Tigre. But it is also true in the secondary, background level of characters, like Admiral Massera, El Tigre's commander in chief, and General Omar Torrijos of Panama. (Dri's wife is Panamanian and, for political reasons and because of personal ties to her family, the Panamanian leader pressures the Argentine Embassy on Dri's behalf.)

This feature of Bonasso's narrative is neither a "mistake" nor an irresolvable defect, although historians and journalists might legitimately doubt its documentary usefulness. Rather, I point it out as the specific rhetorical strategy Bonasso uses to increase the sense of narrative reality of his account. As the dramatist

Alberto Adellach states in his presentation on the back cover of the book:

> Bonasso paints the hidden face of the horror that one lived with in Argentina with a surprising and overwhelming authenticity. He leaves nothing to fiction, because when he takes up people's thoughts, the subjectivity of the protagonist or the hotel room where an agent of repression pursues his pitiful eroticism, he grounds himself securely on verifiable recollections of those who have lived what he describes and who preserve it in the pain of their memory.

> (Bonasso pinta la cara oculta del horror que se vivió en la Argentina, con una precisión que sorprende y una autenticidad que subyuga; sin librar nada a la ficción, pues cuando se mete en los pensamientos, en la subjetividad del protagonista, o en el cuarto de hotel donde un represor ejerce su lastimoso erotismo, lo hace sobre bases ciertas, sobre recuerdos verídicos de quienes lo han vivido y lo conservan en el dolor de la memoria.)

The two phrases, Adellach's "pain of their memory" and Bonasso's title, *Souvenir of Death*, are the elements that justify the narrative. Rather than any specific historical fact, the account strives for an effect, an impression of reality on the basis of its evocation of the signposts of a collective experience of which Dri is projected as the epic embodiment: his escape from the forces of repression is a figure of the ultimate liberation of his countrymen, and, of course, *Souvenir of Death* could only appear when that liberation was a reality.

VI

A substantially different perspective on the Malvinas conflict is provided by a team of political editors of the prestigious Buenos Aires daily *El Clarín*. Clearly the work of trained investigative reporters, *Falklands: The Secret Plot* is an absorbing narrative based on research and interviews. Where so often such events result in "quickie" compilations that may be of short-term interest for the secret information they purport to reveal, closer scrutiny often betrays shoddiness in composition and coherence. The work of Oscar Raúl Cardoso, Ricardo Kirschbaum, and Eduardo van der Kooy does not suffer from such deficiencies, and the impressive publication record it has had—more than a dozen printings within six months of its original release in September 1983—is hardly the result of its aiming for the yellow journalism market. Although it is not a scholarly interpretation of the conflict, nor does it intend to be,[8] one may accept it as a reliable and authoritative discussion of the issues and personalities involved in President Galtieri's ignominious military adventure.

The subtitle leaves no doubt as to the basic rhetorical strategy pursued: the goal is to set forth in detail a "trama secreta" that characterized Galtieri's bid to figure as a national hero and to shore up his shaky power as a national leader. For *Falklands* promotes as its central thesis how Galtieri's decision to retake the Malvinas by force was not simply the result of impatience with the long history of fruitless negotiations with Great Britain: these negotiations were by now a constant inherited by a succession of modern Argentine presidents. Galtieri was determined not to be merely another in a long line of army generals become presidents. Rather, his personal ambition was to succeed Perón as a charismatic national leader and to fill the leadership vacuum created by Perón's death. Although Galtieri had as little use for the Peronista movement as he did for the leftist guerrilla movement that the military exterminated at such great cost to the nation, it is clear that he firmly believed his bold action in the Malvinas would allow him to forge a national consensus that the Peronistas felt was their unique destiny and to assuage the divisive impact of the military's dirty war. *Falklands* makes clear how both goals were doomed to failure.

The narrative quality of the Cardoso–Kirschbaum–van der Kooy presentation of the events of the Malvinas war results from a series

---

8. Cf. Roberto Etchepareborda, "La bibliografía reciente sobre la cuestión Malvinas."

of rhetorical principles: (1) assuming and undertaking to demonstrate that the Malvinas adventure was motivated by Galtieri's personal political ambitions; (2) arguing that the enterprise was tragically flawed by ignorance: Galtieri, his fellow military leaders, and the advisers they chose to listen to miscalculated the response of Great Britain, other Latin American nations, the United Nations, unaligned Third World nations, and the United States; (3) revealing information, formulating interpretations, and asserting judgments that permit a sort of dramatic irony which the authors are privileged to develop in a way in which the "actors" in the event itself (Galtieri and others) were not; (4) mediating between Galtieri's arrogant *triunfalismo* (triumphalism) and the public demand to know the full story of an episode that national leaders misrepresented. Historians, political leaders committed to one point of view or another, and the many individuals mentioned in *Falklands* are entitled to disagree vigorously with the information provided by the authors, in the spirit of free journalistic inquiry. While a criterion of truth, accuracy, and fairness must be applied to *Falklands* by virtue of the sort of document it pretends to be, my interest here is not in verifying its story but in assessing its rhetorical strategies.

Falklands is permeated by recurring ironic motifs based on the principle that it is telling a privileged story. The advertising band that accompanies the edition cited here announces the goal, "In order that the propaganda of the victors not be turned into the official story of the vanquished" (Para que la propaganda de los vencedores no se convierta en la historia oficial de los vencidos). The first irony of *Falklands* occurs with the use of the words *vencedores* (victors) and *vencidos* (vanquished). This pair of forms belongs to the disingenuous byword of the Revolución Libertadora of 1955 that overthrew Perón. Although the promise was made that there would be "neither victors nor vanquished" (ni vencedores ni vencidos) but rather an evenhanded national consensus, historical events soon proved the hypocrisy of the slogan. Thus, one might immediately conclude that the goal of the report by

Cardoso, Kirschbaum, and van der Kooy is to tell the story of the Malvinas war from the point of view of the Argentines (the *vencidos*) so that the British point of view (that of the *vencedores*), which prevailed early on in the non–Latin American international press, might not be the only version told. Yet it becomes clear that *Falklands* is not interested simply in contrasting Argentine and British interpretations of the war. Although considerable documentary information is provided that allows the reader to weigh the different diplomatic, political, and strategic principles involved, it is clear that the reporters have not set out to replace a putative official British history of the war with an Argentine one. Rather, the juxtaposed terms *vencedores* and *vencidos* can only refer to the military dictatorship and the Argentine citizenry. Having vanquished the people through the imposition of a military government, the *vencedores* undertook to extend their conquest to the Malvinas with the goal of prolonging their regime. What Cardoso, Kirschbaum, and van der Kooy report is the failure of that undertaking, the process by which the *vencedores* become the *vencidos*.

Thus, *Falklands* is based on the privilege of irony that results from both hindsight and access to information, documents, and sources that can be collated and analyzed in a way that Galtieri and his government were unable or unwilling to do. As a consequence, the dominant strategy of exposition is the reference to how a circumstance or event understood in one fashion must, in the light of information Cardoso, Kirschbaum, and van der Kooy have been able to establish, be seen in quite another way. This is the classic circumstance of dramatic irony: we in the audience know more about what is going on than do the actors in the drama. If *Falklands* tends to portray Galtieri and the military in general as bumbling fools, it is as a result of the superior information that the authors put forth as rhetorical trump cards. In the following quote, the word *scene (escena)* is used twice. The word echoes the fact that Galtieri has insisted that Alexander Haig return to his hotel by helicopter rather than by car as planned. Galtieri intends that the theatrical spectacle of the assembled multitudes in Plaza

Mayo in front of the Casa Rosada impress the American mediator with the determination of the Argentine people.[9]

Time and again through the detailed chronicle of events, the authors juxtapose the beliefs of the military as to the course of the war with what they have been able to determine subsequently (127, 221, 301 inter alia). The strategy of juxtaposing what "they [Galtieri and the military] thought they knew then" with what "we [the journalists] now know to have been the real facts and the inevitable outcome of events" is not simply a gesture of journalistic superiority. Certainly, the authors of *Falklands*, like any reporters, are justified in getting as much as possible out of the hard work they have done. Rather, it confirms eloquently how ill-informed Galtieri and his government were for the operation they undertook. But the real importance of the rhetorical strategy of *Falklands* lies with the contrast between the image of a controlled and manipulated press during the weeks of the conflict and the free and open reporting the book's authors are now able to engage in. When Galtieri is struggling to retain power after the surrender to the British in the Malvinas, he attempts to stifle criticism of his actions, first through police repression and then through verbal threats:

> When the tear gas still floated above the center of Buenos Aires, Galtieri appeared on television to give his version of the capitulation. The man who was still President roared: "There will be no room for speculation nor deceit. Idle talk is fraud, and any attempt to take advantage of the situation is an insult to the blood of those who fought, and defeatism will be considered treason."
>
> His message was clear: no one could cast doubt on what had been undertaken by the high command during wartime. That would be treason.
>
> (Cuando los gases lacrimógenos todavía flotaban sobre el centro de Buenos Aires, Galtieri se asomó al televisor para dar su versión de la capitulación. El todavía Presidente bramó: "No habrá lugar para la especulación ni el engaño. El ocio será una estafa. El

9. O. R. Cardoso, R. Kirschbaum, and E. van der Kooy, *Malvinas, la trama secreta,* 154, hereafter cited parenthetically in the text.

aprovechamiento de la situación, una injuria a la sangre de los que combatieron, y el derrotismo será una traición."

Su mensaje fue claro: nadie podría poner en duda lo actuado por el alto mando militar en la guerra. Eso sería una traición.) (310)

These sarcastic words synthesize the numerous references to Galtieri's self-seeking management of information during the war. If during his presidency it was impossible to question the decisions that were taken—if it was impossible to posit alternate information or to propose contrary interpretations—publication of *Falklands* is the opportunity to speak with a voice that the censorship of military dictatorship had silenced. The authors, echoing the words of the book's advertising band, go on to speak of the need to counteract the effects of propaganda and of how, despite the inevitable limitations of their information, they are supporting a posture toward events that has not always been possible in Argentina.

Falklands is a fascinating narrative not only by virtue of the journalists' claim to more authoritative information but also as a consequence of the opportunity to defy the censorship that had previously controlled and distorted the news to the benefit of blind personal ambition. The defeat of the Argentine military enterprise and the collapse of Galtieri's government is what makes *Falklands* possible, rather than just the parallel personal ambitions of a trio of political journalists. It is their word against the military's, and the silencing of the latter by the outcome of events created the setting in which *Falklands* could appear.

VII

Daniel Kon's *Los chicos de la guerra* (The boys of the war, 1982), easily the most widely sold of the documents examined in this study, also makes use of the interview format. Eight young conscripts are interviewed at length, and the number of copies sold—more than forty thousand in eight printings from mid-August 1982 to January

31, 1983, the date of the printing quoted here—demonstrated the Argentine public's desire to hear what these young men had to say about their experiences. Moreover, a film version, released in late 1984 with the interviewees as advisers, promised, with limited success, to repeat the popularity of Kon's book. Indeed, the title of the book has assumed the status of an epithet in postwar Argentina.

The first thing to remember about Kon's book is that, like Gabetta's interviews, it was published prior to the nation's return to democracy. After the conclusion of the Malvinas conflict, the military had become as discredited as an armed force as it had become by early 1981 as a government elite—and, to be sure, there are few who do not believe that the invasion of the Malvinas was a desperate attempt to restore Argentine confidence in the generals. As a consequence, and although many writers were quick to take advantage of this discredit to defy official censorship and speak out, the more cautious understood that there was no way to predict how the military would react to public humiliation. Gabetta published his interviews in France, but *The Boys of the War* was brought out in Argentina, and it is for this reason that the soldiers remain partially anonymous, identified only by their first names.

The eight young men—really, boys would be the more appropriate designation, and Kon repeatedly alludes to the boyishness that can still be perceived despite their harsh experiences with war—are a convincing cross section of the conscripts. They come from various parts of the Buenos Aires metropolis and from the provinces, they were generally quite young and unworldly, and their backgrounds range from professional to working class. All but one served in the front line of the war, experienced the combined hardships of the weather and the incompetence of their country's war machine, and saw fellow combatants die. All accepted with youthful and uncritical patriotism the call to serve their country, yet all but one (Carlos was still able to maintain an unswerving commitment to the church and, by extension, to the military that it endorsed so enthusiastically) returned with feelings of bitterness and resentment toward the people under which they served.

Clearly, one cannot apply a criterion of reliability to Kon's interviews. All of the interviewees naturally saw the war from a very limited perspective and, although there is a certain repetition between their accounts (Kon reasonably tended to ask them the same questions) that enables one to consider them representative of all Argentine soldiers in the Malvinas, it would be impossible to confuse their conversations with political or military analysis of the conflict. Kon sought no more than to take the measure of the feelings of those on whom devolved the brunt of the war, and it is here that the main interest of *The Boys of the War* as sociopolitical commentary lies.

In the first place, it is clear that these soldiers, all in their very early twenties, are members of the generation in Argentina that grew up during the succession of military dictatorships beginning in 1966; all would have just entered their teens when it became evident that the Peronista triumph of 1973 was but a prelude to the confirmation of the right-wing military rule that has been the norm during the past two decades. Kon chooses not to discuss this circumstance directly, but his questions concerning the feelings of the men toward their country and its future and toward the often stated assertion that the younger generation lacks commitment constitute clear allusions to the somber social and political situation of the country.

Although *The Boys of the War* may be read as a series of direct statements by a group of representative young men about their combat experiences, there can be little escaping the fact that their comments had considerable resonance for a collective Argentine consciousness that extends far beyond their self-absorbed point of reference. It is understandable that these eight men were obsessed by their individual feelings and actions. Kon interviewed them within weeks of their return, and his questions dwelt primarily on the details of their personal stories. Moreover, the defeat of the war, the discovery that food and clothing had been ineptly distributed and that some superiors had actually hoarded provisions for their own comfort, and their excellent but condescending treatment at the hands of the British during their repatriation naturally contributed to a less than sanguine point of view.

Thus, although the subtitle of Kon's book stresses the question of personal testimonial—"Hablan los soldados que estuvieron en las Malvinas" (The soldiers that were in the Falklands speak)— the natural and spontaneous speech of the soldiers is considerably mediated by the contextualizing operations of Kon's reportage— his own comments, the organization of responses, and the juxta- position of the words of the various informants. It is not so much a question of the material Kon writes to frame the book as a whole and to introduce the individual interviews, nor is it the matter of his questions, which are hardly a model of probing journalism. Rather, *The Boys of the War* must be read inescapably against the backdrop of both the dirty war prior to the invasion of the Mal- vinas and the information about military incompetence during the conflict that had begun to emerge the minute the hostilities were officially over. In this sense, the repeated references to the lack of adequate clothing or food, to the sense of having been abandoned by superiors, and to information provided to them by their British captors become less a litany of grievances about the ill-prepared Argentine war effort than a series of very telling allusions to the cynicism of a military apparatus that made the entire country an instrument of its ambitions. Perhaps this aspect of Kon's interviews does not materialize for those readers who remain inalterably sup- portive of the generals, but one is hypothesizing here that *The Boys of the War* is meant to strike a responsive chord among a disaffected populace, irrespective of the specific feelings of the young men interviewed. It is in this respect that Kon's document is much more than a series of personal statements. There are two consequences from the foregoing circumstances of contextualization. The first is that *The Boys of the War* represents the truth about the Malvinas conflict as told by those at the bottom of the military hierarchy. The second is that the truth inherent in their stories must be read as a counterpoint to the official and self-serving reports of military propaganda, which was meant to deceive both the soldier in the trenches and the civilians back home as to the true course of the war. References to these twin circumstances constitute a dominant thread that runs throughout the interviews.[10]

Kon's document closes with the words of a soldier identified as T., words that constitute a testimonial to the abiding sense of disorientation experienced by the returning soldiers. To be sure, the acute problems of maladjustment of Kon's interviewees are no different than those of the survivors of any war, and modern European and American literature records some very powerful treatments of the subject (Hal Ashby's film *Coming Home* ["Regreso sin gloria"— return without glory—in Spanish] was, not surprisingly, banned in Argentina). The impact of *The Boys of the War*, however, must necessarily be appreciated in the double context of the dirty war and the absence of armed conflict in Argentina's recent history. Argentina had not experienced war since the time of the Guerra de la Triple Alianza in the mid–1860s, and military mobilization was a completely new experience for the national consciousness. Moreover, the loss of young Argentines in the Malvinas can, without much effort, be seen as a perversely logical extension of the roughly ten thousand citizens (a conservative estimate) who lost their lives in the name of the military's efforts to "reorganize" Argentine political life. Both of these circumstances provide contextualizing referents for *The Boys of the War* and add levels of resonance for T.'s unanswered questions that go far beyond the transparent story of the "soldados que estuvieron en las Malvinas."

VIII

Writers quite naturally feel that one of the primary justifications for their efforts is the fact that they are giving voice to individuals, groups, or sets of experiences that might not otherwise be heard. This is especially evident in the motivation behind three emergent categories of writing in Western literature in recent decades: ethnic

---

10. Kon, *Los chicos de la guerra*, 104, 121, 222.

minority, feminist/women's, and gay and lesbian writing. Authors, real or implied, and narrators join forces to avow a commitment to the dignity of a certain segment of human society, and to the value of discovering and promoting that segment. Yet even in general terms, any writer must necessarily feel, as a motivating commitment to the social cause of literature, the need to conceive of the arduous task of composition as serving to legitimate if not the subject matter itself then a particular view of it, whereby that view is constituted by one social network.

In the case, however, of writing under and against tyranni- cal social oppression—what has come to be called contestatorial or resistance literature (literatura contestataria)—writers may well consider themselves spokespersons for society at large, all of whose interests have been dramatically circumscribed or silenced by the dynamics of oppression. While different subclasses or groups (based, for example, on religious or sexual preferences) may face different forms of oppression, the writer under the sign of oppres- sion may begin with the premise that she or he is speaking for all of humanity, to the extent that no viable form of cultural expression is possible within the confines of censorship and all that term evokes.

Of course, even under censorship to any of the degrees of its imposition short of total silence, someone's voice may be heard, only if it is nothing other than that of the group that is controlling the mechanism of censorship in the first place (and, quite often, engaged in creating a discourse to justify its imposition). But the issue is a more profound one than merely that of who gets to speak under tyranny and how many voices get silenced by the many strategies of censorship (and it must be recognized that censorship quite often functions in a less than systematic fashion, such that self-censorship, out of fear, becomes the most prevalent sort of silencing). Rather, what is involved is the idea of whether or not any significant, decent sort of human expression takes place. The belief that none of the speaking that is allowed to take place can ever be meaningful (at least, not in an immediate sense, al- though it may be recodified in terms of various "unintentional" or connotative meanings) is what provides the impulse to create strategies for a contestatorial writing, and what encourages the hypothesis that it is only this sort of writing that can speak in any authentic way for all of society by virtue of the simple fact of its existence, regardless of what its specific overt messages may be. In this sense, an undifferentiated society in its totality (including even the mechanisms of tyranny, which cannot speak its own nature as tyranny but which can only characterize itself disingenuously, thereby also silencing its real self) is viewed as articulating itself via a contestatorial expression and not just as representing the interests of a particular group or "worldview." This circumstance explains why writing under tyranny so often involves something like a global or totalizing expression, lacks the specificity of an expression that is oriented toward the interests of discrete groups, and is likely to appear rapidly dated once the sociopolitical circumstances it describes no longer exist.

Santiago Kovadloff (1942) exemplifies this view of writing against an imposed tyranny of silence. In 1983 Kovadloff published a collection of his essays concerning sociopolitical oppression in Argentina during the 1976–1983 dictatorships. *Argentina, oscuro país: ensayos sobre un tiempo de quebranto* (Argentina, dark country: Essays on a time of rupture) gathers together fourteen texts, in three topical sections, that appeared in various Buenos Aires publications during this period. Thus, in one sense these essays at the time of their writing and publication constituted direct challenges to the structure of censorship both that motivates them and that they defy, while retrospectively they constitute a reflection on a circumstance that has been putatively abolished by the return to institutional democracy. *Argentina, Dark Country* appeared in the series "Memoria del tiempo" ("Memory of time") of Torres Agüero Editor, an important publisher of contestatorial writing, and it is only one of an extensive inventory of post–1983 books in Argentina to survey and analyze the sociopolitical and historical issues associated with the recent military dictatorships and the transition to institutionalism. It is no surprise that Kovadloff, like so many members of his profession and of successive generations of Latin Americans who literally risked their bodies in order to speak their minds, should subscribe to a utilitarian concept of writing in terms nurturing human solidarity. Nor is it surprising, given my introductory comments, that the scope of his essays is wide, in the sense that they pretend to address the entire panorama of recent sociopolitical events in Argentina—a fact made even clearer by the three headings under which he groups his fourteen texts: "La siembra del terror" (Sowing terror); "Malvinas: la guerra de los ciegos" (Falklands, the war of the blind); and "Perspectivas: entre la ética y el garrote" (Perspectives: between ethics and the gallows).

But what does merit highlighting is the affirmation, which is to a great extent a projection of the commitment to the entire panorama of sociopolitical events, that the essayist attributes to his discourse the very configuration of reality. If "reality"—viewed either in the semiotic terms of a reality effect, what the decoding subject agrees to accept as reality, or in the historicomaterial terms of "what hurts"—is what is suppressed, erased both by censorship and the refiguring of the social text by a tyranny that eradicates signs uncongenial to the restricted meaning it functions to impose, the text of the essayist is both the overcoming of silence and the reconstitution of reality. That is, it is not sufficient to restore the voices that have been silenced by tyranny, voices that the essayist sees as in part being channeled through his assumption of speech in the name of human solidarity.

Rather, reality, to the extent that it has been dismantled by the discourse of oppression (and one will recall that the etymon of the word dictatorship is "to say"), must be configured all over again, not merely recovered but essentially reconstituted through the efforts of the spokesperson to reground social discourse in its verbal manifestations in the lived experience of a society. Kovadloff, like many of his colleagues (and not only Argentines in 1983, but those throughout Latin America writing against tyranny or upon the occasion of the restoration of institutional legitimacy), views the writer's obligation to be to rearticulate the social meanings that have been pared away by the process of "dictating meaning."

The twin postulates of meaning suppressed and meaning dismantled are pursued in one of the most eloquent texts in *Argentina,
Dark Country,* "Los chicos y la dictadura" ("The children and the
dictatorship"). This essay is predicated on the implied assumption
that parents are the primary agents of socialization of their children, part of a network of values concerning the bourgeois family
that Kovadloff in another context might wish to challenge. This
process involves not only teaching them about the meanings of
their social world but also inculcating in them strategies for dealing
with what is contradictory, confusing, and even threatening in that
world. Although all social orders are arguably based on ideological
codes that reveal internal contradictions, we do not have to resign
ourselves to the pessimistic or even cynical belief that all social
orders are functioning hypocrisies in order to share the author's implied proposition that the military government can only pursue its
goal of "reconstructing" Argentine society by propagating deceitful
social meanings that both distort the real or deny its existence.
The consequence of this latter operation is that parents, as the
reduplicators of social meaning for their children, are left with
a reserve of meanings about how the world operates—and about
how it has operated to generate dreadful new meanings—that they
cannot account for without dire consequences to themselves and
their children.

Kovadloff's parents must, with guilt and chagrin, reduplicate
the government's mechanisms of oppression: if the family is a
microcosm of society, the tyranny and censorship that exist at the
top of the pyramid of power are effectively reproduced on the
humble if vital level of the family, where the fear of challenging
the discourse of the dictatorship requires its begrudging repro-
duction. Some parents will engage enthusiastically in this project
of reduplication, and one can attribute to Kovadloff's essay the
implied, and therefore unanswered, question as to what a metric
of compliance to the dictatorship's rule of meaning might look like.
His presumption of an ethic of committed human solidarity would,
of course, suggest that the question is impertinent, perhaps even
ingenuous. Yet it does not stretch the imagination to believe that

there were parents eager to reproduce the ideology of the military tyranny on the level of the family, abetted by those who were willing to accept the rules of whatever sector was in power without question, as a strategy for survival. On the other end of the spectrum would lie those who were determined to openly challenge the dictatorial text and to assume the consequences for themselves and their family, although it is not unreasonable to believe that few would be willing in effect to bring their children to the attention of the apparatus of terror in the name of social honesty, with the result being that the internalized norms of parental responsibility in Argentina led most parents to instruct their children in how to stay out of danger, perhaps not always even giving them a complete picture as to what that danger was. Perhaps, by virtue of their own colonization by the agents of dismantled meaning, these parents were at a loss themselves to envision that danger in anything other than vague parameters. It is precisely the function of contestatorial writing, within the outlines of Kovadloff's professional ethics as described in his preface, to counter those agents, to offer adequate profiles of the danger, and to suggest ways in which it can be met and dealt with in the present or at a later time of institutional legitimacy.

As receptors of a dismantled reality that their parents can only allude to apprehensively (if they do not endorse it self-satisfiedly, as victims of an official discourse wildly disconsonant with the lived social text that it has not yet brought completely in line with its reconstructive program), the children of Kovadloff's essay experience all the dyslexia of individuals unable to make sense out of the sign system confronting them: its discontinuities, its aporias, its fragmentariness, and, quite simply, its semiotic inadequacy that leads to the confusion and alienation that are the dysfunctional by-products of the regime's processes of meaning:

> No, there was no reason for the children to know anything. Besides, what did one have to do with what was going on? One had done nothing. They weren't going to touch one. After all, those who were disappearing must have been involved in something, if

it was true that they were disappearing. Yes, the best thing as far as the children were concerned was to ignore it. If one of them asked a question, if one of them suspected something, it was best to be categorical: "That's just things people say. Nobody knows anything for certain. Anyway, it doesn't concern us, and nothing happens to those who are not involved.

And that was that. For just an instant, the children would stare at the drawn faces of their parents and they would catch the severeness with which they were spoken to. Then they would slowly turn their attention back to the steaming spoon in mid-air.

(No, los chicos no tenían por qué saber. Uno, por lo demás, ¿qué tenía que ver con lo que pasaba? Uno nada había hecho. Con uno no se iban a meter. En algo debían andar, al fin y al cabo, los que desaparecían, si es que era cierto que desaparecían. Sí, lo mejor, con los pibes, era dejarlos a un lado. Si alguno preguntaba, si alguno sospechaba, convenía ser rotundo: —Todas esas son cosas que se dicen. Saber, nadie sabe. Nosotros, por lo demás, no tenemos nada que ver. A los que no tienen que ver, no les pasa nada.

Y eso era todo. Por un instante, los chicos miraban fijamente las tensas facciones de sus padres; palpaban en sus corazones la severidad del tono con que se les había hablado, y luego — lentamente— volvían al humeante cucharón sostenido ante los labios.)[11]

Kovadloff's description of a scene between parents and children on the topic of rumors of police brutality is so ironic that it borders on the sarcastic. But what it communicates is how these confrontations between inquiring children and fearful adults meant not only a call to silence, but also the proscription of a dialogue of truth over what was happening and the need to ensure that the children would not commit the foolhardiness of taking their questions to external authority figures like their teachers, the parents of their friends, or churchmen. It meant also the echoing of the commonplaces of the official accounts of the dirty war against subversion: that it had nothing to do with "decent" people, that people were

11. Kovadloff, *Argentina, oscuro país: ensayos sobre un tiempo de quebranto*, 42, hereafter cited parenthetically in the text.

not really "disappearing," that reports of brutality, torture, and assassination were vile calumnies propagated by the enemies of the fatherland. To highlight the anxiety of the scared adults as they repeat these disingenuous formulas, Kovadloff finds it necessary to attribute to the children a perhaps even innocent superiority, as they "read" the subtext of the tension manifest in their parents' faces and sense that they are being betrayed because they are not being told the truth by those whom they have been instructed to trust as the most reliable sources of truth. The consequence of this process of fear-inspired reduplication of the official accounts turns the parents into naive accomplices of the system of repression, in addition to being betrayers of their children's trust and accomplices of the system of repression (43).

The motif of silence that is the principal motive for Kovadloff's writing is displaced, in the need to increase the rhetorical volume of his exposition, by the theme of parents as accomplices of the official text by virtue not of their silence but of their mouthing the cynical explanations designed to produce silence in the children. Concomitantly, the authorial voice functions to bring about both a retraction of that silence (assumed by the parents, imposed on the children) and a revision of the cynical version of events by offering the author's superior knowledge of what must be said within the framework of the *república constitucional* (constitutional republic). The *"servilismo cívico"* (civic servileness) attributed to the accomplices of the regime is erased and overwritten by the contestatorial discourse assumed by the author.

The tenor of these comments is not meant in any way to undermine the legitimacy of Kovadloff's essay or of his authorial voice in general. Indeed, it would be difficult to imagine what other discursive strategy Kovadloff might adopt in the effort to configure the sociocultural consequences of the combined processes of silence and distortion of the official text and to propound a corrective analysis of an adequately grounded historicomaterial reality. The task for the essayist is to find a way back into historicomaterial reality that can expunge the interpretive record of the prevarications of the tyrannical text. By appealing to a presumed clean-slate innocence

of these intimidated witnesses to their society, the rhetorical strategies of "The Children and the Dictatorship" result in an especially
eloquent essay. Kovadloff's writing ingratiates itself by proposing
to be a starting point whereby the defiant challenge of these questions can ultimately be formulated.

Kovadloff's most recent published collection of essays, *Por un
futuro imperfecto* (Toward an imperfect future, 1987) contains a text
that appeared originally in 1984, "La guerra de las voces" (The
war of voices). The essay speaks of the vociferous cacophony to
be found in a society in which commonality of opinion is overlain
by willfully different voices of alienated individuals. This *estruen-
do yo* (thundering I) has been liberated by return to institutional
democracy and the removal of the constraints of silence described
in *Argentina, Dark Country*.[12] Yet it is clear that this cacophony is
no more productive of a sense of historicomaterial reality than the
official versions that can now be so loudly denounced. Thus, in this
new context the authorial voice must once again reconfigure itself
to pursue the project of speaking a sociopolitical text that has yet to
be delimited—hence, the clever trope of a morphological category
that provides the title of this collection. In the closing paragraph
of the title essay, which is also the closing paragraph of the collection, Kovadloff, with an entirely fresh set of disjunctive categories
provided by the newly reconstituted Argentine public discourse,
charts the space that now must serve to justify his commentary,
which promotes the incessant processes of definition and analysis,
the opposite of a discursive practice that can only lead back to
the categorical rigidities of the tyrannical text he had previously
sought to contest.

Read today, almost twenty years after the initial events they portray the essays discussed in this chapter could seem dated. But
this is less a consequence of the time frame to which they refer
and more a result of the potential to see them as suspending,

12. Kovadloff, *Por un futuro imperfecto*, 83.

so to speak, political disbelief. The intertwined commitment to revealing the truth about the terrorist state and to making, directly or by implication, a call for the reform of military institutions constituted a determining factor in a cultural production that saw the 1976–1983 military dictatorship and the process of institutional redemocratization to emerge from it as a watershed of Argentine social history. This attitude is nowhere more eloquently expressed than in the report of the Argentine National Commission on the Disappeared, *Nunca más* (Never more, 1984), headed by the distinguished novelist and essayist Ernesto Sabato. This report took its name from post-Holocaust culture, and it strove to evoke many of the same profound resonances.

Nevertheless, it would be rather rash to imply that these writers were turning their gaze away from the dynamics of a complex, ongoing society such as Argentina's. Subsequent writings by these and other journalists, which make up an impressive inventory in the long and distinguished tradition of the journalism of social analysis in Argentina, make it clear that no illusions were ever entertained about the possibilities of reshaping the character of the institutions of power. Certainly, such essays cannot be read only as symptomatic of an attitude of the moment—euphoric optimism or grim resignation—vis-à-vis national realities. The Proceso created a particular space for cultural production, one that is not strictly chronological, and these writings were some of the texts enabled by the existence of that space. As such, attitudes toward the Proceso, who was involved and how they were involved, and how the Proceso should or should not continue to serve as a point of reference for contemporary Argentina, will necessarily continue to mark the collective consciousness and its individual expressions, which is certainly one reason texts such as these cannot be read as only confining their meaning to a receding decade, whether one understands that decade to be the historical period of the Proceso or that of the subsequent period of redemocratization. Moreover, it can be argued that, especially with the deaths of Julio Cortázar (1984), who continues to be the largest-selling Argentine writer, Jorge Luis Borges (1986), and Manuel Puig (1990), there is no reigning giant of Argentine literary culture, with the possible exception of Ernesto Sabato, who has in reality been silent as a writer for twenty years. The consequence of this sort of "vacuum" is to perpetuate the sensation that Argentina is continuing to experience a period of cultural transition. While indeed that period may extend indefinitely, abetted by the postmodern distrust in literary giants, it serves to maintain the cultural production of the Proceso as an inevitable watershed of national consciousness, one that is both eloquent and grandiloquent, exceptionally pertinent to current events like the Menem presidency-by-degree and unfettered neoliberalism, or regrettably outstripped by them.

CHAPTER 2

Argentine Fiction during the
Proceso de Reorganización Nacional

There is no ethical or political reason not to recognize that Argentine literature existed in exile during the years of the Proceso, or that many important writers such as Julio Cortázar (who had lived outside of Argentina, in any event, since the 1950s), Manuel Puig (whose separation from Argentina had occurred during the military dictatorships of the mid-1960s), and David Viñas published major works abroad, especially in Spain and Mexico. One cannot deny that there were writers who fled Argentina between 1976 and 1983 who wrote novels that tended to center themselves in the lost homeland or in a personal life experience that synthesized the historical course of national events. At times, these works received applause and awards for their intrinsic qualities, as well as for their testimony of a Latin American phenomenon that also served as commentary on a general Latin American situation.

The simple truth is that not all of the Argentines who left the country did so only because there were more opportunities abroad or because the Argentine institutions and corporations for which they worked suffered profound modifications. Of course, there were those who left for this reason and those who went for yet another one: intimidation and terror speak with many voices and come in many shades. For a large number, there was neither the time nor the conditions to think through the situation calmly or carefully.

In this manner many fled, defending themselves the best they could in circumstances that were less than kind and, in general, terribly painful. The scant successes of the few who had, to a small degree, triumphed did nothing to inspire or relieve the pain of those who, for better or worse, chose or were forced to live outside the country. Consequently, this reality confirms the fact that Argentina's major product of export for many years was its own citizenry.

This, however, does not mean that there is any inclination to confer upon the exiles the virtue of serving as the guardians of national culture. This attitude implies that any lack of a nucleus of Argentines abroad involved in sociocultural activities would represent the disappearance of national identity. Of course, the matter becomes complicated when one remembers that there have been writers in exile who have had at their disposal the system of the free press, along with the safeguards of the constitutional rights of freedom of speech in the countries where they took refuge. Part of this freedom implied the possibility not necessarily of self-promotion, but of access to the entire spectrum of opportunities in order to articulate concerns from one's own lived situation. These opportunities included professorships, participation in academic conferences, and the lack of concern over the impingement by censorship and tyranny on what one attempted to accomplish by distancing oneself from such censorship and tyranny. Inevitably, those who did not enjoy a complete understanding of all the facts of the situation jumped all too quickly to the conclusion that they had the privilege of harkening to an Argentine culture sheltered by exile. (Note must be made here, in all fairness, of the thousands of individuals who experienced exile—laborers, skilled workers, and many professionals—without any of the subsequent "glory" attached to the circumstances of artists and intellectuals who had access to multiple public forums.)

Whether or not exile imposes a distinct imperative to write in a certain style and whether those authors that write and publish while in exile do so in a different manner, are questions that involve subjective criteria. Undoubtedly, writing in exile permitted a certain tranquility of knowing that one was protected from the "environment of persecution." But at the same time, there was the realization that each day one was further removed from the texture of Argentine daily life with all its horrid and frightful crevices. It is that life that had been left behind to assume the pathetic—but not tragic or cynical—condition of being exiled.[1]

However, fairness to the exile who wrote about the condition of being Argentine (and indulging in the misleading temptation of believing that this writing naturally coincided with Argentine literature of the period) cannot mean that one must continue to speak of an Argentine literature in exile as if it were a proven, indisputable fact. Even worse would be to insinuate that the Proceso demanded a categorical bifurcation between literature of exiled writers (writing that could speak strongly, freely, and genuinely) and literature written under the dictatorship (that could only speak with the timidity and fear implacably imposed by the tyranny).

The greatest injustice is to believe that no culture existed in Argentina between 1976 and 1983. Even though it may be true that this culture suffered from all the inequalities caused by dictatorship, such an unevenness may have been, in large part, more the result of the priorities favoring the multinational corporations than the inflexible practice of censorship. Censorship always functioned erratically and according to the momentary personal mania of the censors, and it never operated with the coherent Draconian political program the exiled writer at times suggested in order to justify being able to write only when far from home. Rather, at issue is intimidation via the "grimaces of fear," as announced by the title of one of the novels of the era that put the system to the test.

The following is not just a statement of the obvious: that the inequities and the silence, the disappearance of publishing houses, of theaters, of galleries, and the sad state of the stock of books in the bookstores and the newsstands were all definitive elements of Argentine culture of this period. That is to say, the lack of original and national culture was what best characterized the internal

1. Luis Gregorich, "La literatura dividida."

panorama. A conversion of those gaps and sectors of silence into the global panorama of Argentine culture within the country can do no less than encourage the idea that Argentine culture existed only in exile.

However, the facts refute the hypothesis that the exile held a privileged status. One would have to examine the overwhelming success of the 1981 Teatro Abierto (Open Theater) movement and the parallel phenomena of Danza Abierta (Open Dance), Poesía Abierta (Open Poetry), and Cine Abierto (Open Cinema). In defiance of the dictatorship and at a rather favorable moment after the Malvinas debacle, these groups were able to demonstrate that not all of the creativity had been exiled or silenced, especially in the case of theater, a true mark of Argentine pride. In fact, the idea of openly vindicating a segment of national culture was the culmination and explosion of the internal pressure that had been building for five years, further propelled with each injustice or arbitrary act in the commercial sector.

The long-established publishing houses as well as the newer ones included in their catalogs the books of writers searching for codes of expression that would allow them to bring to their readers an interpretation of what was happening in Argentina. More than victims of direct repression—and there had been publications directly banned and confiscated—they were victims of indifference and fear. Whether the problem was the extent to which the Argentine middle class did or did not know what was going on or whether this group preferred to look the other way (the characteristic cautionary slogan was "don't get involved"), the modes of communication that survive on the short-lived tastes of the middle class made it possible to avoid giving an adequate account of its production. Disdainful ignorance was more efficient than direct censorship and, by contrast to their colleagues in exile, the writers and artists from within did not enjoy the mechanisms of open societies that would allow them to make themselves heard: as far as I know, it has never occurred to anyone to organize an academic congress on Argentine culture not in exile.

Someday someone will write the documental history of the radio programs that dared to interview the *non sancti*. The history will be written of how the best forum for sociopolitical commentary was a gutsy humor magazine, *Humor registrado* (Copyrighted humor/Humor on record), and of how theatrical representations of foreign works became interpretive performances of national issues. It will be the story of the blooming of daily newspapers that had, at times, little mass distribution, but whose particular cultural interests transcended the purely national. The story will be about the literary and criticism workshops that functioned on the margins of the institutions to preserve and stimulate those elements that the institutions, thanks to their corruption by the military, were ignoring. It will tell of all the clandestine cultural projects that, precisely for being concealed, did not attract the attention of the international community that had come to believe that the brain waves of the Argentine cultural body marked a fatal, uninterrupted horizontal line.

When democracy returned and when the cultural establishment began to struggle to modernize, while also fighting to be audaciously involved in the process of redemocratization, it became surprising to see just how much had been produced culturally in Argentina during the seven long years of the Proceso. The inventory may not be exactly worthy of the myth of Argentine culture, and it may not cover the appreciable ravages of cultural continuity caused by the dictatorship. However, what cannot be denied—and what Argentines cannot discredit—is the valor and the dignity of those who, against wind and sea, worked so that theirs would be contestatorial voices within the country in the name of the majority of the Argentines who had no other option except to remain behind during the Proceso.

Yes, there was literature written in exile. But a nation that brought to justice the generals of the juntas can no longer conform to the appeal of the privileged optic of those in exile. The writers and artists who returned from exile—and not all could or wanted to—were constrained to express a debt of gratitude for the welcome from those who, with much pain and at times great personal sacrifice, sustained and supported Argentine culture from their native soil. The argument over who suffered more is, in the final analysis, as nonproductive as it is destructive. As David Viñas (one of Argentina's most brilliant writers and a man who lost two children to the dirty war) said so well, Argentines must stop throwing stones at each other.

A strictly classificatory approach to the narrative production of the period of the Proceso is unnecessary. Neither would a rigorous evaluation of the artistic significance of the works be of much value, whether these are defined in terms of continuity of transnational criteria of literary originality or postulated in terms of an adhesion to an ad hoc inventory of what should have been the recoverable writing of the period. A much more appropriate approach, from my point of view, is to identify a number of works that respond to various sociocultural pressures of the period. These pressures are postulated in terms of the possibilities of expression within the prevailing political system, and they respond to the varied requirements of metacultural interpretation within the system.

With parameters of classification and critical judgment suspended, we are able to go directly to the core in terms of the writer who, during this period, stands out as a synthesis of the cultural formation imposed by the Proceso and as a most defiant gesture to it. Enrique Medina already has to his credit a list of approximately twenty works of fiction. This is a production of approximately one book per year since his first book, *The Tombs*, in 1972, a work which made a definitive break with the decency and euphemism characteristic of Argentine literary production. Given that *The Tombs* pertains to another stage of tyrannical military administrators in Argentina, it inaugurates, with its crude language and its unavoidable metaphor of Argentina as a sadistic prison of minors, a narrative vein that Medina would continue to develop throughout his long trajectory of banned and censored works. Within this production are visible lifestyles not seen simply as static aspects of an atemporal Argentine social structure, but rather as the excrescence of the dynamic rhythm of degradation imposed by the political machine. The Proceso "restructured" much more than it was desirable or even possible to admit, and the unfortunate derivations of this production are what Medina proposes to bring to light in his novels.

As there exist so many novels, we will avoid the casually informative listing of titles and themes. It is sufficient to say that these works range from the most widely sold titles by an Argentine author to ones that received the least amount of attention from the guardians of the social morality. No less than eight of these books were sequestered in some way in the period from 1976 to 1983; not until in 1983, barely a month before Alfonsín assumed office, was official censorship lifted.

For the purpose of characterizing one of the novelistic modes during the Proceso, no other work of Medina would be more appropriate than *El Duke* (*The Duke.*) Published in November 1976, eight months after the establishment of the mechanisms of repression, *The Duke* was banned in January 1977. Subtitled, in the 1984 edition, "Memorias y anti-memorias de un participante en la represión" (Memoirs and anti-memoirs of a participant in the repression), *The Duke* is the story of a former boxer who works as a hired assassin for parapolice groups. He himself ends up eliminated by them in a destructive, spiraling whirlwind that forgives nothing nor no one. The epigraph that serves as a prelude to a narration of amazing degradation suspends all subtlety in setting the parameters of society as a bloody ring:

> JUDGE *(impatiently)*: Did you know that your rival was in bad shape when you hit him at the end?
>
> WORLD BOXING CHAMPION *(haughtily)*: Your honor, my job is to leave my adversaries in bad shape.[2]
>
> (JUEZ *[impaciente]*: ¿Usted sabía que su rival estaba en malas condiciones físicas cuando le aplicó los últimos golpes? . . .
>
> CAMPEON MUNDIAL DE BOX *[altivo]*: Señor juez, mi negocio consiste en dejar en malas condiciones físicas a mis adversarios.)   (1)

2. Translation from the English version, *The Duke*.

Following *The Duke,* Medina studied in depth the variants of the unsurmountable wall of violence and social rape during the military's dirty war with a series of annual titles that appear to have been written to tighten, one after another, the screws of the apparatus of censorship: *Perros de la noche* (Dogs of the night, 1978) denounces, among other things, the pornographic movies that according to some versions were converted into one of the most lucrative and valued export products under a government that promoted the sacred Catholic institution of the family and legendary Western values; *Las muecas del miedo* (The grimaces of fear, 1981) projects the kafkaesque image of hidden forces that scare us, sometimes systematically, sometimes chaotically, with grimaces of fear that are like a grotesque totalitarianism of underdevelopment; *Con el trapo en la boca* (With the gag in her mouth, 1983), in which a "Proceso girl" (the phrase comes from a review in the *Buenos Aires Herald* written at a time when the venerable English language daily was fighting the dictatorship as part of a British anti–Argentine campaign) speaks with a language acquired in life experiences that combine militarism and macho bravado in one system, resulting in a disarticulation of the dignity and morale of the individual. Medina closes the cycle of his novels with a work that deals with the impact of daily life on someone of the masses of the port of Buenos Aires during the Proceso. In his short story collection, *Los asesinos* (The assassins, 1984), the title text takes place in the consciousness of a worn-out starlet/whore. There, the configurations of society whose children (incarnate in the newborns taken from the arms and uteruses of the political disappeared) are converted into charity-fair prizes for the accomplices of the regime.

One of the most notable characteristics of Medina is how he amplifies the range of the typical Argentine novel, in which the focus of interest very seldom includes women (and when they are included, it is to serve as a point of reference for the masculine conscience).[3] From that tradition, novels like *Dogs of the Night* and *With the Gag in Her Mouth* and short stories like "The Assassins" install the perspective of the narrative discourse in the feminine conscience to approach a situation of a feminist commitment to the issue of marginal women. These women are the last in a long line of individuals screwed by society; they, in turn, screw their most vulnerable neighbor. But attention must be paid to the female narrators of the period, to see if these confirm this interpretation of their participation in the social scheme, and to observe whether they restructure this system to tell their own version of things.

undoubtedly, it had to be Marta Lynch who most successfully attracted attention in this respect, not only for her inventory of titles of some editorial success during the period being considered here, but also, more importantly, for the complexity and ambiguity of her position in relation to the network of power. Lynch basically identified with the moral right, which was able to contemplate with nobly feigned horror the "excesses" of those novice sorcerers who had been trusted with society's sociopolitical well-being. She drew an outline of narrative in Argentina in terms of a social strata of women who have nothing to do with the lowly outcasts who populate the pages of Enrique Medina's books.

La penúltima versión de la Colorada Villanueva (The penultimate version of Colorada Villanueva, 1979) portrays a decent woman from an upper-middle-class district who has been abandoned by her husband and her three children. They leave the country either for personal reasons during a moment of economic and institutional crisis, because they fall victim to the repression, or simply because internal exile is easier than breaking affectionate ties at a moment when such ties are a luxury that no one can afford. Lynch structured her novel around the consciousness and the interior monologue of Colorada, a discursive strategy that stands out as a primary characteristic of her novelistic style. Her narrations are limited to women who make use of available resources to be able

3. Cf. Francine Masiello's reservations about this strategy, "Cuerpo/presencia."

to think about their own lives.[4] What emerges is a sketch of a certain sociopolitical reality relative to the sentimental and emotional peculiarity of the protagonist, a slanted articulation that allows no space for doubt regarding the contradictory events being rehearsed in a woman's mind. This, meanwhile, saves the writer from the uncomfortable experience of the loud screaming or alienation that would leave her without a discursive center. Shortening the distentions of the narrative allegory, Mrs. Villanueva is Argentina, and this role foresees the honorable awakening of consciousness of the upper middle class that Norma Aleandro portrays in Luis Puenzo's movie *La historia oficial* (The official story, 1985; the filmscript was written by a woman, Aída Bortnik, whose dramatic work was included in the Teatro Abierto movement, and thus this text also can be seen as seeking its space in the feminist versions of the Proceso).

Given the fact that Argentina is one of the richest Latin American nations in regard to female narrators, there is no lack of names that could be considered here as exponents of interpretations of the Proceso. Perhaps Griselda Gambaro is the most forceful, at least in terms of the solidity of the postulates of her narrative and the audacity with which she assumes the imperative to speak, without ambiguity, about the structures of power and the dynamics of the repression that form part of the Argentine social code. *Ganarse la muerte* (Earning death, 1976) is one of the many versions by Gambaro of the microcosm of the family seen as an axis of institutionalized degradation (one will remember the pieties about the family uttered by the demagoguery of the Proceso). The reaction of the censors to this novel, which was confiscated for its contempt of the sacred institutions, was one of the motivations that impelled Gambaro to spend the greater part of the period living in Barcelona. There, she complemented *Earning Death* with *Dios no nos quiere contentos* (God does not want us happy, 1979). This novel retraces facts about the social system to postulate a

---

4. Naomi Lindstrom, "Women's Discourse Difficulties in a Novel by Marta Lynch."

governing principle in affront to the official ideology. Barcelona is also where Gambaro wrote *Lo impenetrable* (*The Impenetrable Madam X*, 1984), an erotic tale that was published only after the restoration of the constitution. Aside from identifying questions about the aspirations of the individual, in the person of an abused woman, these novels mark a significant change in the direction of Gambaro's creativity. She likes to respond to the question of why her dramatic texts abound with male characters by saying that this was due to the simple fact that the questions demanding consideration dealt with masculine domination. However, the three works mentioned here focus on female protagonists as recipients of aggressive acts.

It seems legitimate to recognize how the women writers are able to assume a peculiar marginal optic without falling into the necessity of dividing literature into categories such as masculine and feminine. From that perspective, female characters created by male writers are of particular interest (as in the case of *With the Gag in Her Mouth* of Medina), or, by the same token, male characters created by female writers. Playing with the double meaning of the word *patient*, Ana María Shúa exemplifies the latter possibility with *Soy paciente* (I'm [a] patient, 1980). Kafkaesque metaphors of bureaucracy and justice as a synecdoche of a pulverizing society are brought to life in Shúa's text, where the atmosphere of the modern technological hospital lends itself to several interpretations. On one hand, the hospital is seen as the axis of the individual's preoccupation with the survival of the body and as a point of condensation for the frustrations of being a number in the face of the anonymity and falseness of technology. Aside from this view, the structure of the hospital allows the exploitation of medical science to be seen as an instrument of terror (compare the clinical images in the theater pieces of Eduardo Pavlovsky in *El señor Galíndez* [Mr. Galíndez] and *El señor Laforgue* [Mr. Laforgue]). This novel is rooted in the reality of editorial circumstances that were not very favorable for a defiant attitude toward Argentine society during the Proceso. However, since signs receive their meaning within the context of their decodification, this image of institutional degradation of human beings does not fail to have resonance within the parameters outlined here.

Another woman writer whose formation is similar to that of Lynch is Martha Mercader. Like *Informe bajo llave* (Report under lock and key), which will be analyzed in a later chapter, *Solamente ella* (Only her, 1981) presents the story of an artist who ends up the victim of a sociopolitical dynamics that she had initially underestimated in her belief that she could manipulate it toward her own ends. The protagonist is a tango singer and her story is set in 1975 on the eve of the Proceso but at a time when the forces of repression are already firmly in place. Along with the discovery of a crime-ridden world existing behind the facade of the national culture industry, the singer learns to recognize the continuities between organized crime and political repression. *Only Her* is noteworthy as a conjugation of feminist and sociopolitical interests in the female character's meditation, "being a woman in Buenos Aires— what a dumb undertaking" (ser mujer en Buenos Aires, pavada de proyecto), an assertion that cuts to the core of Argentine myths about independent women in control of their own lives.

If texts like the foregoing can be read as narrativizing fragments of the Argentine social text, then historical dimensions provide an additional resonance by offering the possibility of understanding events in terms of long-standing constants embedded in the national unconscious. Concomitantly, a historical dimension allows for the meaningful reinscription of the apparently harmless local color phenomena of the past in the context of dramatically contemporary events that they are seen to prefigure. Mercader makes use of both of these parameters in *Juanamanuela mucha mujer* (Juanamanuela, quite a woman, 1980), which deals with the nineteenth-century writer Juana Manuela Gorriti. The result is the image of a woman whose scandalous life constituted a stridently demythificational reading of her repressive society in both its social and its political dimensions. (See the same sort of revisionist reading of the life of Camila O'Gorman, who was executed alongside her lover, a priest, in 1848 with the acquiescence of her father, to be found in María Luisa Bemberg's 1984 film, *Camila*.)

The historic dimension, especially in what is implied in a revisionist reading of the official texts (one can refer to the professor of Argentine history in *The Official Story*), is echoed in *Respiración artificial* (*Artificial Respiration*, 1980) by Ricardo Piglia. Here, events rooted in the two extremes of Argentine history are blended together to insinuate a continuity of lies, deception, and corruption in a society where the utopian dreams of the searchers after mysteries vanish in the presence of the prevailing dystopia. Piglia is known for his forays into detective fiction, a genre that seems to constantly renew itself with new dimensions in Argentina. If *Nombre falso* (False name, 1975) involves a collection of stories unabashedly in the style of Chandler and Hammett, the formula crime-mystery rests directly on the bases of the violence of Argentine society, and *Artificial Respiration* appeals to the reader-investigator whose successive readings uncover repeated transformations in a single historic account. Whereas North Americans are startled by a center void of meaning or where the meaning is the fraudulent move to cover this void (the list would begin with Thomas Pynchon and include writers such as Ishmael Reed, Gore Vidal, Robert Coover, and E. L. Doctorow), a novelist like Piglia takes on a history all too dense and omnipresent in its reverberations of inescapable configurations (hence, the vast panorama of revisionist history found in the novels of David Viñas, whose project responds more to a liberal mythology of Argentine social history than to his radical version within the ideology of the Proceso).

The ideology of the Proceso demanded defining the norms of Argentine society within very narrow parameters: a society that rested on the Christian and Western values of the Sacred Institutions of The Fatherland and founded on the intransigent persecution of these same values. As a consequence, any exception made to the text of power serves, at least at first, to reinforce the image of an oppositional and disruptive literature. Needless to say, we cannot limit ourselves only to searing versions like those of Medina, or even less so, to the type of meticulous deconstructive analysis of the prevailing "ideologems." *Cuerpo a cuerpo* (Body to body, 1979) is one such example. Viñas published this novel in Mexico, and its text stands out as a focal point for the inquiry into Argentine fiction written in exile during this period. It serves to legitimize, for the objectives of this essay, those texts that otherwise would appear insufficiently engaged with the points of reference of the sociopolitical reality.

The combination of putative sexual "immorality" (lesbianism) and the bitter vision of the monumentalized institutions (specifically, the teaching profession) meet head on in Reina Roffé's *Monte de Venus* (Mount of Venus, 1976).[5] The censorship applied to this novel and to others that defy a Mother's Day vision of the Argentine family puts in check the attempts to explore this subject. This check gives even more resonance to those works that were able to find such a voice. But *El beso de la mujer araña* (*Kiss of the Spider Woman*, 1976) by Manuel Puig was published abroad and *De tales cuales* (One and the same, 1973) by Abelardo Arias pertains to the illusion of a short period of creative effervescence, following the three 1966–1973 military governments and prior to the definitive cruelty and viciousness of the dictatorship inaugurated in 1976.

La brasa en la mano (The live coal in the hand, 1983) by Oscar Hermes Villordo came out in the bookstores and newsstands only at the end of the period of military rule. The novel was protected in part by the author's position on the editorial staff of the newspaper *La Nación* and in part by the futility of censorship at that moment. It deals with homosexuals, harmonizing a chorus of voices and interior monologues that sketch one of the most decentralized aspects of Argentine society. The text postulates a biting repudiation of the healthy self-image of the metropolis, where one of the imperatives of the repression has been to cover over the multiple faces of sexual desire with a facade of bourgeois decency. Villordo attempts to naturalize a spectrum of defiant behaviors by way of their exposition in a literary text. This is accomplished by unabashedly portraying how a group of individuals pursue, with an unconventional naturalness, their unique styles of living and by postulating a harmonious relationship between public and

5. Foster, *Alternate Voices*, 76–81.

private values that legitimize the former while contemptuously denouncing the latter as being irrelevant and useless. In this way, *The Live Coal in the Hand* confirms the existence of a marginal underworld that official moral Argentina attempted historically to deny. At the same time, this negation extended itself to an entire panorama of palpable social realities. Much less than a scandalous text in terms of what is represented therein (that is to say, there are no large-scale erotic scenes), Villordo's text constitutes a panorama of experiences marked, like any other, by the memory of suffering, loss, disillusion, and frustration.[6]

The Live Coal in the Hand finishes with a Petronian banquet that fits into the novel as the contrary image of the institutions of decent society (in this case, the eloquent dinner as conforming ritual) and as a carnivalesque vision of the degrading and degraded societal norms. The free-for-all, as an alternative to the overwhelming official seriousness of the official image of decent Argentine life, was an attitude strongly promoted by Julio Cortázar. From the point of view of Argentine social history, it could be said that the unifying thread of many aspects of the vast zones of marginated culture have to do precisely with variants of Rabelaisian carnivalization of social norms. For this reason, during the Proceso enterprises such as the magazines *Humor registrado* and *Superhumor*, both published by Ediciones de la Urraca, directly experienced sociopolitical reverberations, suffering all the accompanying aggressions and persecutions. The novelist Luis Rafael Sánchez spoke once of "a poetics of the obscene" as a necessary corrective to the disconcerting decency of Puerto Rican society.[7] The same concept is applicable in Argentina in the works of certain authors.

It is regrettable that criticism has focused so much on *Flores robadas en los jardines de Quilmes* (Flowers stolen in the gardens of Quilmes, 1980), partly because the novel is lamentable and partly because it does not exemplify the predominant tone of Jorge Asís's fiction. Besides its very serious tone, *Flowers* casts the image of

6. Foster, *Gay and Lesbian Themes*, 72–76.
7. Luis Rafael Sánchez, "Apuntación mínima de lo soez."

the young people's protest as a mere trendy pastime. The only option for the disillusioned and cynical postadolescent ends up being integration into the system. We could stop here to meditate on cynicism as the ultimate refuge for Argentines faced with the monolithic system of national life as refined by the Proceso. But that would be at the expense of resignation to the inevitable, a dead-end street that repudiates, with the dignity and the courage of its writing, most of the writers mentioned above. All of Asís's work might be sealed under the cynicism that is something of an Argentine vice (does the novelist confirm it or does he restrict himself only to reporting on it?). The greater part of Asís's texts immerse themselves in the variants of this cynicism with a strong, playful, carnivalized tone that makes them pertinent to this investigation. *Los reventados* (Fucked up), originally published in 1973, caused more of a stir in its 1976 version. The series inaugurated with *Carne picada* (Chopped meat, 1981) produced an extensive panorama of the period. Also to be mentioned is *Cuaderno de Oberdán Rocamora* (Oberdán Rocamora's notebook, 1977), the not so felicitous modernization of the optics of Roberto Arlt's *Aguafuertes porteñas* (Buenos Aires etchings). I lack information about a totally carnivalesque version corresponding to the period of the Proceso (even though they existed before the Proceso—see *Guía de pecadores* [Sinners' guide, 1972] by Eduardo Gudiño Kieffer—and after it— *Bazar de 0.95* [Five and dime, 1984] and *Kermese* [Bazaar, 1984], by Geno Díaz). This absence, and the unsuccessful attempts of Asís, of course, say a lot about the conditions of expression between 1976 and 1983.

I will avoid closing this commentary with a list of other writers whose works I would like to or should analyze. The criticism on Argentine literature always oscillates between the desperation provoked by the enormous editorial production of the country in even its worse economic and political moments and an attitude that tends to discard almost everything as passing and clumsily imitative. The simple fact is that many great works of Argentine fiction are the fruit of exile, and this must be accepted as one of the outstanding facts of national culture. But the novels published in

Argentina during the Proceso cannot be looked at contemptuously as texts irremediably scarred by the impossibility of an adequate expression of national life. Undoubtedly, yes, many suffered from the profound ambiguity resulting from the circumstances of writing and publishing under tyranny. There is, however, great value and valor in the mere fact of having the desire to sustain the social function of fiction under the shadow of a terrorist state.

CHAPTER 3

Rape and Social Formation

Enrique Medina's *Las tumbas*

The need to understand a complex social situation underlies the construction of literary microcosms; this need is social to the extent that it sustains the collective circulation of culture, and individual in that it explains one use individuals make of culture. By this one refers only indirectly to the way in which the "fictional world" is a microcosm of reality in the sense of a documentary miniature, a sort of easily comprehensible outline. This it most certainly is, and no matter to what degree the writer follows an imperative to strive diligently for a sense of the vastness of the social fabric and the nuances of personal behavior within it, the narrative can never be more than a coded map of the actual reality of social experience and the historical dynamic.[1] In a more specialized sense, then, an appeal to a hypothesis of the narrative as microcosmic must be in response to the ways in which the so-called fictional world is *not* meant to insinuate a coextensiveness with society as a whole. Instead, reference is being more properly made to narrative fiction as metaphoric, or synecdochical, of whatever may arguably be felt as the larger, real-world social fabric. Narrative as microcosmic metaphor or synecdoche—A is [the same as] B or, less ambitiously, A is a singularly representative component of B—is an

---

1. My general theoretical frame of reference is Fredric Jameson, *The Political Unconscious: Narrative as a Socially Symbolic Act.*

attempt to represent social experience by discovering a shorthand that can evoke it.

Such an evocation is a form of shorthand because the process of narrative construction engages in strategies of containment. Paradoxically, in order to posit a limited fictional world—one that is limited necessarily, we may say, by the representational shortcomings of narrative itself or of whatever other ascetic epistemology we may wish to appeal to—that bespeaks broader social panoramas, fictional narrative "contains" (holds in check or inhibits) the process of signification. This containment of signification occurs whenever the shorthand is unambiguous and internally coherent. Thus, an "allegorical" novel like *Alice in Wonderland* is internally coherent and microcosmic to the extent that the reader perceives how the realm down the hole, no matter how reduced in its dimensions, is really the whole maddeningly contradictory and seemingly arbitrary world of our daily social experience, and to the degree that all of the fictional elements brought into play contribute to reinforcing this "message" with a minimum of semiotic slippage. Were the text, viewed either as an identifiable structure providing the conditions of meaning or as a process involving author and reader as the producers of meaning, to be judged as ambiguous or "open," internal coherence would be seen as concomitantly reduced and the boundaries of its microcosmic state would be seriously challenged.

Whether a particular text may "intend" to be microcosmic, and therefore constrained in its semiosis such that the internal coherence of its microcosmic quality may be apparent, is a question of specific ideologies of interpretation and critical reading. These ideologies may choose to see all narratives as necessarily microcosmic and then proceed to take to task those in which the strategies of containment are demonstrably ineffectual, with the result that it is not clear what society, what aspect of society, or what social dynamic is being symbolically rewritten via the narrative codes. Or such ideologies may strive to identify a specific form of textual production in which microcosmic encoding is chosen

by writers as particularly well suited to their engagement with
history and the cultural project of interpreting it through narrative
reenactment. Whether these narrative reenactments are microcosmic because social history is too vast to grasp in any other fashion
or because of the peculiar symbolic potentialities of a carefully
circumscribed semiotic process, so that a sense of internal coherence leads comfortably to desired attitudes and interpretations,
is an open question, one that has in large measure to do with
whatever authors, readers, and critics/theoreticians will decide to
believe about the function of literature in determinate moments
of history.[2]

Microcosmic narratives have been prevalent in the Argentine
narratives of the past twenty years. Some of these narratives can
be called allegorical in the strict terms of a network of signifiers
whose meaning is secondary rather than primary.[3] Since the social
experience under military tyranny and under various guises of
repression (even during moments of alleged freedom of expression)
cannot be expressed in bald terms (that is, the daily signs used to
articulate it, however fragmentarily and even hypocritically, cannot
be employed in cultural documents perceived to be about or in juxtaposition to daily experience), an alternate code must be sought.
This code must be sufficiently different in order to serve as "original" or "creative," yet transparent enough to permit the recovery of
the daily code that has been suppressed. In this case, the secondary
code of the allegorical text is, in fact, some register of the daily code,
while the primary code, the superficially attributable meanings of
the created text, is in fact the one that is "secondary," in the sense
of having been fabricated in place of the already present code that
must, however, be suppressed. Novels that report events in strange
countries or even other worlds (for example, science fiction as a
paradigm of allegories of repression), or narratives in the much
vaunted Argentine fantastic, now whimsical, now grotesque, are

2. Terry Eagleton, *Literary Theory: An Introduction.*
3. Foster, "Traspasando los géneros literarios."

engaging in encoding practices where a ground zero of "social documentariness" cannot be the basis for textual production.[4]

By contrast, when narrative social documentary reemerges in Argentina with the return to institutional democracy, it is particularly aggressive in "calling things by their right names" in apparent response to allegory and the inexpugnable stain of repression that it bears within its very nature as overtly, even triumphantly, displaced discourse. One may define these allegorical narratives along different axes and derive different inventories, suitable to different interpretations of the relationship between cultural production and the society of military tyranny in Argentina. Certainly, nothing is to be gained by viewing all narrative as allegorical, nor by engaging in a process of "translation" that moves, in correlative gatherings of meaning, between primary and secondary codes such that no debris of unaccounted signs is left over, even when the conditions for recognizing the allegorical are cast in such a way that there is a high degree of agreement as to the presence of interacting primary and secondary codes. It is enough for the moment to recognize how the cynical vagaries of cultural repression in Argentina in recent decades generated a variety of textual modes that fit comfortably under the umbrella of allegory and that, at some moment of cultural redemocratization, an aggressive mode of social documentary emerged to take their place, superseding them as a consequence of the shame of the circumstances of cultural repression that they are condemned always to witness by their very existence.

Yet the dynamics of narrative encodings viewed along a continuum between allegory and social documentary do not really have much to do with the microcosmic as a metaphorical or synecdochical relationship between the fictional and the social worlds, unless and only if it is that allegories, because of the ad hoc nature of their primary (that is, extranarratively secondary) sense, are inescapably constrained: the imagination of the writer is never as vast as that of overall society and its multiple complex codes of self-

4. Emil Volek, "Summary: Semiotics of Literature under Pressure, Aesthetics and Pragmatics of the Argentine Novel in the 1970s and 1980s."

representation. Viewed in this fashion, the microcosmic narrative is not really an allegory of society at large, but rather a semiotically contained representation of it where the specific conditions of representation do not constitute the juxtaposition of two correlated codes but rather textually determined conditions on the use of fundamental social codes that can only be partially gathered into the text.

It is most assuredly in this fashion that one would want to view that particularly original Argentine dramatic form, the neo-grotesque (neo, in order to distinguish it from its European, expressionistic antecedents). Rather than fictional worlds whose signs must be translated back into those of historical reality, the grotesque plays of these dramatists, from at least Armando Discépolo and Roberto Arlt through the Teatro Abierto movement of the last years of the Proceso, are microcosmic stages in which the actual social dynamic of Argentine society is assumed in its own terms, albeit with the properly rhetorical highlighting needed to make the qualifier "grotesque" applicable.[5] Indeed, the one essential point about these plays is that historical reality is so horrible that its daily dimensions outstrip escapist fantasies of the grotesque, that the gap between averred morality and actual social practices is so vast and so hypocritical that it can only lead to a conduct of human affairs which, when seen from the distancing vantage point of cultural texts, can only be qualified as grotesque. Admittedly, there is a relative metric involved here, but the agreement to call these works grotesque yields to the imperative to work back from the term in order to understand what perception of social reality is at issue, from the allegation that society never works in the ways in which its public morality asserts it does, to avowals that a society's self-serving myths have become so hypocritical that a radical quality like the grotesque has become naturalized to the point of no longer even calling attention to itself—at least, not until cultural production then undertakes to do so in its deconstructive rearticulations. When this occurs, what the grotesque frames or

5. Claudia Kaiser-Lenoir, *El grotesco criollo: estilo teatral de una época.*

what is viewed as grotesque is a microcosm of society at large, one ideologeme of which (as in the case of the ideologeme of "hacer la América" in Roberto Cossa's paradigmatically grotesque play *La nona* [Grandma, 1978]) is used as the generating principle of a text's production, a production in turn circumscribed or contained by the internal coherence of the shorthand brought to bear on the controlling ideologemic principle or element.

In the case of Enrique Medina's *The Tombs*, a cause célèbre of contemporary Argentine fiction,[6] the principle of microcosmic narrativity can readily be appreciated in terms of the foregoing parameters. It does not take much imagination to understand how a prison narrative functions as a portrayal of society at large. In the American consciousness, such narratives are particularly associated with a film genre of the 1940s and 1950s, and while many of the pertinent titles were part of the efforts to distinguish a specifically criminal culture in the United States as part of a renewed law-and-order campaign after the social blurring of the Great Depression,[7] there is in many of these works a homologizing undercurrent whereby continuities between prison and the world, the microcosm and the macrocosm, emerge. Although Genet-like attempts to radically invert the semantic poles between good and bad in prison narratives are rare, it has not taken much subtlety to discover how the institutional "correctional" structures in prison narratives are merely a most efficient version of the general corruption by the society that maintains them. Indeed, the idea that prisons only maximize the corruption of the individual begun by a cynically immoral world is enough of a sophomoric truism that the only originality that may attend to it are narrative proposals regarding how any measure of human dignity survives such a conjunction of the forces of dehumanization—as, for example, in Puig's *Kiss of the Spider Woman* and in Héctor Babenco's 1986 movie version of the book.

6. Juan Bazán, "Enrique Medina"; cf. Bella Jozef on the occasion of the Brazilian translation, "Enrique Medina, o tempo sem recuperação."
7. Eugene Rostow, *Born to Lose: The Gangster Film in America.*

The enormous repudiation of Medina's *The Tombs* by official and semiofficial sectors such as the church, traditional academic critics, and a cultural establishment committed to an elitist definition of art, plus the fact that it was banned by the military government and remained unavailable between 1977 and 1982, are facts that have little to do with how the novel depicts life within a correctional institution as a more efficient version of the external corruption that maintains it. Arguably, few have any illusions about the corrective value of penal institutions, and, official declarations aside, one can assume as a working hypothesis that readers would assume places like the Tombs exist to warehouse incorrigible individuals and that the forms of violence involved in that warehousing are necessary attributes of a system that society cannot do without. It might not even be too difficult to discover a consensus to the effect that society (blamed for being "modern" and alienating) exercises pressures on the individual to be bad and to do evil, which fortunately most of us are able to resist as we go through life; those individuals who succumb to these pressures, perhaps through little fault of their own, must regrettably be restrained so that our world is not made worse than it already is. I have no sociological research on which to base this proposition of a basic agreement about social life among the readers of narratives like *The Tombs* or its many varieties in American culture. But history has been harsh enough in Argentina for one to believe that it is not far-fetched to postulate as a common point of reference the hypothesis that, upon mature reflection about our social life, prisons are necessary nightmares. As a consequence, to construct a narrative around intertwined propositions that prisons enhance the corruption of the individual by society, that they corrupt the innocent (whatever the concept of social innocence might be), and that the notion of their being "correctional" masks the real role they play (warehousing the noxious by-products of specific social processes) does not represent a particularly daring undertaking.[8] From at least the time of the first success with readers of *Les*

8. Michel Foucault, *Discipline and Punish.*

Misérables, all but the most cynical members of our society can see in the prison inmate some measure of social victimization.

To a large degree, the difficulties Medina experienced with *The Tombs,* his first published work and only the first of eight that were subsequently to be banned, one after the other, during the 1970s and early 1980s, were those encountered by virtually any cultural product during the military tyranny that adopted even the most modest stance of critical skepticism toward the dominant ideologies the junta found it advantageous to sustain. (It must be noted that some of Medina's works were also banned by the nominally institutional government of María Estela Martínez de Perón.) It has been well documented how any reservation, any analytical stance toward values like the family, (Catholic) tradition, or the (patriarchal) fatherland, within the overall practices that are generally denounced as "neofascist," ran the risk of repression and censorship.[9] In Medina's novels, one of whose unifying motifs has been the denunciation of the hypocrisies of Catholic morality in both its general versions and in the more narrow constructions espoused by the neofascist military, one could not help but run afoul of the efforts (often only semiofficial) in Argentina to control culture. No one among those wielding power over culture could have been happy with the equation linking the world and the reformatory in *The Tombs,* but that equation cannot have been the primary reason for its denunciation.

Nor can it have been the consequence of the novel's emphasis on the juvenile reformatory rather than an institution of adult corrections. Although Argentina shares in the prevailing Western belief concerning the sanctity of childhood, the innocence of the young, and the imperative to provide appropriate safeguards against the evils of the world, Buñuelesque views about the abiding presence of the amoral *olvidados* (the forgotten)[10]—fundamentally a rewriting of the antimoralizing postulates of the Spanish picaresque—

9. Avellaneda, *Censura, autoritarismo y cultura.*
10. The reference is to Buñuel's 1950 film, *Los olvidados,* released in English as *The Young and the Damned,* about the youths caught in the urban poverty of midcentury Mexico City at the beginning of its intensive phase of modern development.

have enough currency such that to maintain the presence of evil
in children is not particularly scary even to the best of hearts, as is
demonstrated by paragons of popular culture beliefs to this effect
like William Golding's novel *Lord of the Flies* (1959) or Maxwell
Anderson's play *The Bad Seed* (1955), works of some pretensions
at literary merit that could be supplemented by a long list of
horror products like Stephen King's novel *Carrie* (1974) and its
avatars. What is interesting to contemplate in a proposition about
inherently good and bad children, a proposition that sets aside
orthodox Catholic/Judeo-Christian morality, is its relationship to
matters of class bias. Whether being the bearer of a bad seed is the
consequence of coming from the marginal classes of society (and
therefore constituting a threat to those who have been blessed by
God with virtue and social position) or whether it is, conversely,
the taint of those born in the stratum of corrupt power whose victims are the humble and honest poor, ideologemes about bad seeds
and congenitally damned souls are built around the reversibility
or bidirectionality of hypotheses concerning moral qualities and
class identity.

The bottom line is that, even in a society under the sway of
beatific visions of the innocence of the young, the sort of relentless
investiture of marginal youths as the standard-bearers of social
corruption that we find in *The Tombs* is more simply unsettling
than it is breathtakingly scandalous. Indeed, one could propose the
hypothesis that the children who populate the pages of Medina's
novel and whose gross exploits, which are one with the harsh
punishments to which they are subjected as the just desserts of
their truancies, are only to be expected, given the social milieu
from which they are drawn. Moreover, if in one context *The Tombs*
can be read as an answer to the social programs of Peronism (and
there is ample collateral information to justify placing the novel
within the context of the culture of Peronism in Argentina in the
late 1940s and early 1950s), programs that were unable to follow
through on their promises of overcoming class conflict and social
margination while at the same time they in fact perpetuated many
of the historical dynamics of conflict and margination, the novel

can also be read as confirming the presence in that society of the very slag heap of degenerate humanity that Peronism exalted.[11] The children of *The Tombs* are *descamisados* (shirtless: Eva Duarte de Perón's metonymy for the dispossessed) whose horrifying behavior only confirms the need to restrain them through institutions like the reformatory and the prison.

If these individuals are social givens, and if we leave aside the rhetoric we can identify in the text for producing one or another meaning about the dimensions of their social identity, then they are susceptible to a variety of contradictory interpretations that may have little to do with the way in which the novel actually uses them. And, as is often the case with novels like *The Tombs*, the popular consciousness (including that of the censors) is often likely to be based on such tangential readings of the text. Thus, in regarding *The Tombs* as a narrative rewriting about the social role of children treated as irrelevant, the legion of urchins in the novel can have been alternately viewed as confirming the failures of Peronism and as supporting the anti-Peronist denunciations of the dangers of exalting the socially marginal and the morally corrupt, quite aside from any competing view of these children as victims of their adult society. As a matter of fact, a reading of *The Tombs*—or, not even a reading, but a general impression held by the community—as unsupportive of Peronism for any of these reasons would correspond to the view of Peronism sustained by the military dictatorship and its supporters: Peronism was one of the major threats to national integrity and security. For all of these reasons, any view of children as unrepentant degenerates that the novel may be argued to promote would hardly have been considered outrageously objectionable, except perhaps only by optimistic social workers.

Rather, it is in the dimensions of sexuality where *The Tombs* has been disturbing to its readers, whether they are the agents of repression or the spokespersons of an aesthetically grounded conception of literature. Sexual abuse and exploitation is not an

---

11. Avellaneda, *El tema del peronismo en la narrativa argentina.*

alien motif in prison narratives or their parallel registers such as boarding school memoirs and madhouse tales. Sexual favors as a reward for collaborating with a structure of power and rape as a punishment for nonacquiescence or defiance recur enough in these narratives to make it clear that sex is somehow intimately related to the larger issue of the social dynamic. Feminist social theory now holds as axiomatic that rape against women is a tool by which the patriarchal society controls women with sexual violence,[12] through the agency of specific individuals who, no matter how much the patriarchy's laws may proscribe rape, are in effect serving as instruments for its harshest means of control. Rape is a specter that reminds women to adhere to confining strictures that limit their freedom and expression in exchange for protecting them from violation (the narreme runs something like "Be a good girl and remain under the protection of Daddy's home or the Big Bad Wolf will get you"). And rape is a way of punishing women who deviate from the patriarchal norm ("She was just asking for it by not dressing and acting like Daddy told her to"; this is, of course, assuming that Daddy is not himself the rapist, or the arbiter of his daughter's licentious costume). Rape involves sex neither as a manifestation of erotica (*pace* illusions about women enjoying being taken by force) nor as a type of moral corruption (positive or negative, depending on one's views regarding sexual taboos). Rather, rape is sex as an instrument for the destruction of its victim.[13]

The fact that the boundaries are confusing if not contradictory between the patriarchal society as protector from rape and as wielder of the instrument of rape for social control is one of the reasons why sexual violence is an especially important phenomenon for understanding issues related to the social control over women. And since feminism must, in the final analysis, argue that those issues in fact relate to all individuals and not just to women, violence, sexual or otherwise, cannot be viewed in any other way

12. Susan Brownmiller, *Against Our Will: Men, Women, and Rape.*
13. Elaine Scarry, *The Body in Pain: The Making and Unmaking of the World;* Andrea Dworkin, *Intercourse.*

than as an instrument generated by structures of domination and not simply as a random happening outside the sphere of social control. Hence, the truism that patriarchal society requires violence to sustain itself, even while it repudiates that violence as the behavior of the antisocial. One of the rhetorical advantages of prison narratives as microcosmic realms (an advantage shared by family romances, as feminist writers have discovered) is that the reduced inventory of signs acquires a greater metaphoric or synecdochical economy in demonstrating clearly the relationship between social control and violence, with rape being the starkest manifestation of that violence. (In all of this discussion, I am ignoring the thorny question of whether sadomasochism is a form of rape, as in John Rechy's *The Rushes* [1979], or whether it is a variety of sexual theatrics between consenting individuals; in the latter interpretation, it becomes coextensive with rape and ceases to be a dramatic form of pleasurable sex when it is no longer based on mutual consent.)

Yet rape is fundamentally different from other forms of violence. Setting aside random phenomena where certain types of violence share a spectrum along with certain pleasurable experiences (force feeding vs. dining; torture by excessive sound volume vs. music), rape involves the inappropriate use of the individual's most basic erotic experience, in which pleasure in the context of personal consent is directly proportional to the role of sex in the preservation of the species. Indeed, if sexual violence is not necessarily any more physically painful than many other forms of assault on the body, the horrifying psychological dimensions of rape are the consequence of the importance of sexuality as both an intense form of pleasure and a biological necessity. Whether the repudiation of rape is viewed as a social construct or as "natural" or as a complicated combination of the two is, of course, important within sociological theorizing. But as a sociological given, the rape taboo can serve in cultural documents, either analyzed or used as simply a convenient sign, to mark what happens at certain points in the social dynamic: given a specific set of circumstances, rape occurs as a consequence of those circumstances. In a feminist narrative, a woman may be raped, as happens to one of the lesbian lovers at the end of Gloria Naylor's *The Women of Brewster Place* (1980), for refusing to accept the primacy of the phallus. In a prison narrative, the failure to accept the authority of the kingpin will inexorably result in the rape of the foolhardy dissident. In some of these narratives, good sex (or at least nonviolent sex) is the reward for collaboration with the system, but it turns to bad sex (rape) when the system is defied, as can be seen in the personal story of an individual whose protection is accompanied by pleasurable sex and who is then punished with rape for a transgression. This is essentially the trajectory of the protagonist in Marta Lynch's *Informe bajo llave* (Report under lock and key, 1983), and good sex also becomes bad sex in the same fashion in Judith Rossner's *Looking for Mr. Goodbar* (1975). Feminist literature involves male-to-female rape as part of examining the ramifications of patriarchalism as a form of violent social control. Prison narratives (or boarding school memoirs) essentially involve male-to-male rape (and there are female-to-female examples like Tom Eyen's play *Women Behind Bars* [1975], although there are fewer texts) because of the same-sex environments involved.

In much of the bibliography that could be cited, rape as punishment (and let us set aside the question as to whether this phrase is redundant: can rape be anything other than a violent act of punishment, no matter how much its agent is isolated as socially deviant?) is usually no more than obliquely referred to. At most, it may figure in a culminating scene of violence where it summarizes all of the violence against the individual that has been accumulating throughout the narrative trajectory, much like the grand finale shoot-out in the paradigmatic Western. This is what happens at the end of Naylor's novel: the macho violence against the lesbian sums up the several strands of dehumanization to which the women of Brewster Place are victims in stereotypic fashion. The same can be said of Rossner's *Looking for Mr. Goodbar*. It is as though the contract for these narratives allows only one major rape scene and as though the impact of that scene would be diluted if it were only one of several. Of course, one could argue that the literal rape scene is nothing more than the culmination of a trajectory of violent and degrading indignities, of partial rapes, as much psychological as physical, that lead up to the full-blown violation, which combines as much emotional lacerations as it does corporal rendings.

It is important to note that one of the founding texts of Argentine literature is Esteban Echeverría's short story *El matadero* (The slaughterhouse, written circa 1841 but published posthumously in 1871). After speaking in unrelentingly graphic terms of the entire context of social violence fomented by the tyrant Juan Manuel de Rosas, the narrative zeros in on a young man whom the mob recognizes as part of the political opposition. Echeverría, who wishes to promote the hypothesis that the mob is the unwitting instrument of the tyrant and its members are his worst victims, focuses on the humiliation of the young man as the "rape" of Argentina by Rosas and his witless agents. Fittingly, the story ends with the death of the man as preparations are made apparently to rape him, in terms that are joltingly explicit for when the story was written.[14] The narrative equation of *The Slaughterhouse* is, therefore, a simple and classically allegorical one: the rape of the *unitario* (Unitarian: a political partisan of a unified, strong central government; opposed by the Federalists) by Rosas's agents is the rape of Argentina by the tyrant, with all of the accompanying bloodletting and indignities Echeverría sees this violent social process as assuming. In a way that would have reinforced this typically allegorical equation, Argentina, as a feminine noun, could have been represented by an innocent maiden exposed to ravishment. By using as a victim a man, a "real-life" representative of the political opposition, allegorical weight is sacrificed, but the impact of the narrative is gained by concentrating political violence in the form of the insinuation of homosexual rape.

The added eloquence of conjoining the rape taboo and the taboo of male-to-male sex (and overlooking for the moment the hypothesis that rape is not a sexual act, but an act of violence, or at least one in which sex, drained of its erotic meaning, is used as an instrument of violence) is what makes *The Slaughterhouse* and,

---

14. Foster, "Paschal Symbology in Echeverría's *El matadero.*"

almost 150 years later, *The Tombs,* particularly jolting. Moreover, Medina, in the pursuit of a recurring image of degrading violence, repudiates any contract whereby there can only be one grand finale rape scene, and his novel is built around the strategic recurrence of rape scenes as harsh harmony to an array of various patterns of violent humiliation in the microcosmic "reformatory." One can, then, see a constellation of reasons, features that we can reasonably assume to have been deliberately chosen and reinforced, to make *The Tombs* such a repugnant novel for readers and censors nervous in the face of any literature that questions the dominant social order and that deviates from a criterion of literature as decorative rather than documentary, and, additionally, from a criterion whereby socially relevant literature must be more symbolic than documentary. The motif of the microcosmic prison; the image of youth as paradigms of the adult world, as victims as well as agents of it; an aggressive register of colloquial language that inventories all of the taboo words of Argentine Spanish; the recurrence of rape in statistical conformance (rather than as only suggestive) with its actual presence in the macrocosm; and the pattern of male-to-male sexual abuse as an utterly unsentimentalizable sign of the unappealable dynamic of violent exploitation: the conjunction of these elements is what guaranteed *The Tombs* its bitter harvest of recriminations and censorship. And it is logical to assume that the generalized sense of repugnance created by the novel is precisely what Medina was aiming for, even when the repugnance is directed illegitimately against the messenger rather than the message. By denouncing Medina and *The Tombs,* as the process of censorship did and as its vestiges continue to do under democracy (if only in officially unsanctioned ways), the reader refuses to face the way in which the microcosmic metaphor is documentarily appropriate and ideologically valid.

Yet ideological validity cannot be ensured for *The Tombs* simply by pointing out that the novel is justified because it provides an accurate microcosmic metaphor of the rape of individuals in numerous ways as the interpretive rewriting of a prevailing social dynamic. Ideological validation requires much more than simply being able to say that a text is "right" in its representation of history. In the case of *The Tombs*, the conjunction of rape and male-to-male sex serves as a major point of reference for the discussion of ideological validity. In pursuing this topic, there can be no question that one has to set aside as totally irrelevant any objections to the discussion of male-to-male sexual activity, since one can neither question whether such activity occurs in places like the Tumbas (either by mutual consent or as a manifestation of violence) or whether homosexuality is a valid form of erotic expression. Indeed, homosexuality, as one of the many faces of eroticism, is not at issue in *The Tombs*, despite the fact that male-to-male sex is involved. Surely, all male domains like the army, boarding schools, monasteries, and prisons provide ample opportunity for the flowering of homoerotic love, just as the world at large provides ample opportunity for individuals to fulfill their erotic needs, varieties of repression and the social control of sex in the name of other communal goals aside. That certain contexts are better suited to pursuing certain erotic needs or that certain contexts encourage the definition of erotic needs in specific ways is not a surprising discovery, and fictional microcosms are in many ways demonstrations of the suitability (or the tragicopathetic unsuitability) of various life contexts for the pursuit of erotic interests: in some cases love (defined as coterminous with eroticism as something complementary to or different from it) flourishes and in some contexts it leads the lover(s) to fatal endings via a number of interpretations of the (im)possibilities of love in historical societies or their subsets.[15] As it happens, the literature on homosexual passion tends to view such love as leading to untoward consequences, a not unreasonable conclusion, given the abiding general tenor of social attitudes—and outright legal and violent persecution—of homosexuality, although it is important to note numerous contemporary revisions of homoerotic passion in terms of providing "positive" models for its prevalence, among them several stories in Medina's *Aventuras de amor prohibido* (Adventures of forbidden love, 1988).

15. Foster, *Gay and Lesbian Themes in Latin American Writing.*

But Medina, who in his fiction has generally pursued the two faces of sex—sex as repression and destruction, and sex as personal liberation in defiance of societal castrations—is not really interested in homosexuality as a face of passion in *The Tombs*, a fact that is completely missed by Juan Acevedo in his denunciation of the novel as antigay. Certainly, Acevedo and gay rights activists have reason to lament the use of male-to-male rape as an act of violence for controlling and punishing the individual, but no more than feminists have the right to lament male-to-female rape as a misuse of heterosexual intercourse as an act of violence. Sex as violence is clearly not the same thing as sex as erotic passion, no more than speaking and eating are the same thing despite their common involvement of the mouth.[16]

What is particularly scandalous about *The Tombs* is not the documentary details of a spectrum of psychological and physical violence to which the inmates of the reformatory are exposed (and which they revisit on their guardians in grim retaliation), but the fact that sexual activity, which happens to be defined only in terms of male-to-male contact (although there are some gestures toward erotic exchanges between the protagonist and female guards), occurs only as controlling and punitive rape, only as the degradation of one individual by another, and never as an erotic impulse of personal liberation. Even when some of the inmates use others simply to fuck (as in the case of the monstrous and moronic Frankenstein), the humiliation of the other is involved and there is never a liberating exchange of erotic feeling. Acevedo—and other readers committed to an erotica of liberation—might wish the image of sex as rape were alleviated by the image of sex as liberation (whether heterosexual or homosexual), but such an out is not possible within the historical world *The Tombs* inscribes. Even if in any real-world reformatory, the overall pattern of sex as rape might coexist with sex as liberation within precarious and hidden pockets of resistance to the reduplicated societal dynamic, Medina's novel, as part of its

16. Zelmar Acevedo, *Homosexualidad: hacia la destrucción de los mitos*, 118–19. Jane Gallop, *Thinking through the Body*, 18–19.

microcosmic synecdochical process, excludes any vestige of sex as liberation in the interests of highlighting the grim nature of that dynamic, which can, after all, only expect to prevail in the end, given the conditions of its historical existence and the integral role it plays in the workings of society vis-à-vis the individual. This is perhaps most eloquently true in the way in which the inmates rebel, not to seek their liberation from repression or their freedom from confinement, but simply to repeat on the body of one of their guards the same humiliating degradation of which they are objects, which is in turn a faithful image of a sociopolitical reality whereby class conflict generates unbroken cycles of revenge and counterrevenge rather than a liberation from oppressive history:

> Gutiérrez wakes me up at midnight.
> The police come.
> The lights are out in our dorm but everyone's sitting on his bed. The dormitory chiefs are walking up and down the hall and talking in a low voice. We see the policeman and the Director go by. Later the Detective, in pajamas, talks with the night watchman.
> The watchman had found Flat Butt in the downstairs hall, hogtied with an enormous carrot sticking out his blood-smeared butt. They had already carried him off to the hospital. . . .
> They took Flat Butt's clothes away and we never saw him again. The general detention included dessert and there was no way to escape that. After a week the rumor went around that Flat Butt was okay and that they'd had to take stitches in his asshole. After two weeks we saw dessert again, all of us. The detention and the discipline started to lax. By the third week we could calmly plan a new escapade on the outside. (171–73)[17]

> (A la medianoche se despierta Gutiérrez.
> Vino la cana.
> En nuestro dormitorio estaban las luces apagadas pero todos sentados en las camas. Los jefes de dormitorios paseaban por el jol y conversaban en voz baja. Vimos pasar a los canas y al director. Después el Detective en piyama hablando con el sereno.

---

17. All translations of *Las tumbas* are from the translation *Las tumbas (The Tombs),* and are hereafter cited parenthetically in the text.

El sereno había encontrado en el jol de abajo a Culo Sentado, atado de pies y manos con una enorme zanahoria enterrada en el orto lleno de sangre. Ya se lo habían llevado a un hospital. [. . .]

Se llevaron la ropa de Culo Sentado y nunca más lo vimos. La encanada general incluía el postre, de ésa no nos pudimos salvar. A la semana se empezó a rumorear que Culo Sentado estaba bien y que le habían tenido que coser el ortito. A la segunda semana volvimos a ver el postre, todos. Las canas y la disciplina iban aflojando. A la tercer semana, con toda tranquilidad pude planear una nueva escapada afuera.)

One will note that the principal concern in this story of the rape of one of the guards with a carrot is that it results in the suspension for two weeks of dessert—a minor inconvenience without further consequences, since the act of violence is apparently not serious enough to warrant any additional action on the part of the authorities.

If to validate the ideology of *The Tombs* it is enough to accept that life in the reformatory conforms essentially with the facts of Medina's representation and that the parameters of the microcosm have a reasonable measure of coincidence with a larger social dynamic, there nevertheless remains the question of the narrative voice in the novel. Medina has chosen to provide access to the world of the Tombs as social microcosm through the agency of a first-person narrator who recounts his own experiences in navigating that world. Of course, it is legitimate to assume that the narrative voice is autobiographical, and there is ample evidence from the information available about Medina to suggest that to a large extent this is so, even though he has repudiated Héctor Babenco's movie version of the novel, *Pixote*, as seriously distorting the experience he records. While the decision to employ a first-person narrative provides authentication in the form of a bridge between the two worlds—the narrator lived the microcosm but installs himself in the macrocosm by being the voice of a cultural text read in the outside world—the narrative is, nevertheless, not unfraught with difficulties.

One of the ideologemes of Medina's novel is that the inmates of the reformatory are not just passive victims of the violence visited upon them in the name of controlling and restructuring them, but that they reduplicate in their behavior the very violence of which they are objects. The object becomes the agent of brutal violence, including rape, because the boundaries between victims and criminals is not clear-cut in the way in which simplistic versions of We versus They would have us believe. The most horrifying sociological fact is that victimization creates new victimizers in a ceaseless chain of reduplication, as investigations on rapists and child abusers have amply demonstrated. This is the importance of the description of the rape of Flat Butt: the raped become new agents of rape. In the second part of the novel, the narrator, now in a new and more efficiently organized reformatory, entertains erotic feelings toward Gabriela by accepting becoming an extension of her arm of violent subjugation, wherein his sexual feelings are directly related to having been a diligent student of the more refined techniques of physical violence that she exemplifies. After the brilliant lesson, she asks him:

> "You like it?"
> "Yes, Missy Gabriela."
> I want to tell her she's great but I start to stutter. She lets her head fall all the way back and her hair bunches up on my shirt. We're in the same position as when she had a hold of the little jerk. Except now she's the jerk and I'm her.
> "What are you saying?"
> "How good you are to me." (295)

> (—¿Estás contento conmigo?
> —Mucho, sita Gabriela.
> Quiero decirle que es muy buena pero me pongo a tartamudear. Deja caer del todo la cabeza para atrás y su pelo se abulta sobre mi camisa. Estamos en la misma posición que cuando ella lo tenía agarrado al pendejito [the object of the lesson]. Nada más que ahora ella es el pendejito y yo soy ella . . .
> —¿Qué decís?
> —Que usted es muy buena conmigo.)

Were the reader to be bothered by the fact that up to this point in the novel, the narrator witnesses and, to a certain extent, participates in the rape of fellow inmates, as though the narrator were outside the world he claims to describe from the vantage point of having participated in, it is now amply evident that the narrator has become fully socialized into the system that the novel is, in fact, repudiating by its relentless, sangfroid depiction of it. In the second part of the novel, emphasis lies less on random rape (in the sense in which it is customarily understood) and more on the systematic, violent abuse of the internees by their female guards; it is an abuse with unmistakable sexual overtones. The guards are presented as sadomasochistic mistresses, much like the fearsome disciplinarian in the anonymous *Harriet Marwood, Governess* (1967) who derives erotic pleasure from vigorously whipping her male charge. The narrator who has himself been on the receiving end of the guards' straps, shrewdly notes after witnessing someone else's correction:

> I had gotten beaten so many, many times and I had seen so many, many beatings that I don't know why the hell I felt those blows like I was receiving them myself. I couldn't stand seeing him writhing on the floor. . . . It made me go to pieces. (312)

> (Tantas, tantas biabas había recibido y tantas, tantas había visto, que no me explicaba por qué carajos sentía los golpes como si me lo estuvieran dando a mí. No aguantaba verlo retorciéndose en el suelo. [. . .] Me cagué el alma.)

> Missy Sarita makes him come out of the shower and knocks him to the ground with a single blow. She carts him off dripping wet and kills him. I suppose it must be just like coming. I suppose that's the case, to judge by Missy Sarita's glassy eyes. (317)

> (Sita Sarita lo hace saltar de la ducha y lo sienta de culo de un viandazo. Se lo lleva todo mojado y lo mata. Supongo que debe ser lo mismo que acabar . . . Supongo nomás, por los ojos vidriosos de sita Sarita.)

The random sexual assaults of the first part have been replaced by a form of systematic, sadistic abuse totally integrated within the institutional structure of social control.

Although the narrator cannot represent himself as the agent of literal rape (perhaps because of the taboos of homosexuality that the early Medina seems unable to deal with, even though such rape does not have anything to do with homosexuality as it is construed as a variety of erotic fulfillment), he is ultimately able to view himself as fully socialized within the essential dominant violence of the Tombs whereby victim and victimizer are one and the same in a pattern of social reduplication, which, to be sure, the very language of the narrative confirms, not only in the use of words relating directly to violence but also in the insistence of an aggressive sociolinguistic register that is indicative of the realms of social margination.

Yet this structure of course does not really work in the novel. For if in fact the narrator does become completely socialized to the dynamic of violence that controls his world, there could be no point at which he could step out and become the narrator of a contestatorial rewriting of the parameters of that world. In order to produce *The Tombs*, the narrator must have been an incompletely socialized victim/victimizer, an incompetent rapist, because otherwise he cannot have attained the vantage point that makes possible the rewriting of the historical text as narrative. But this is exactly what happens: at the end of the novel, the narrator walks away, as Medina claims to have walked away from his real-life experience as a reformatory inmate, subsequently to become the author of *The Tombs.*

This ending is anticlimactic because it introduces an element of structural failure at odds with the compact continuities between raped and rapist that are developed throughout the novel and that culminate in the apprenticeship to the female guard Gabriela, with all its erotic overtones. Medina's narrator wants to have it both ways, to be a thoroughly socialized participant in the world of the Tombs (since by becoming a full-fledged rapist he demonstrates the terrifying economy of that historical system) and to be the spokesman for a stepping back from that dynamic in order to frame its function as a microcosm of personal humiliation in the name of social control. It is not immediately apparent if this adds up to a contradiction in the ideological sense of the novel. But if this is, in fact, contradictory—the narrator as victim versus the narrator as a superior documentary voice—it is perhaps a contradiction not of the structure of the novel but of the social text it reenacts: we are all products of a system of social determination but we cling to the possibility (illusion?) of a cultural production that can transcend the circumscriptions on self-reflection imposed by the humiliation of violence.

This brings us back to the theme of containment: microcosmic narratives wield various strategies of containment, otherwise they would be coterminous with the confusing flow of daily life. In order to be rewritings or interpretations of daily life, it is necessary for the narratives to contain the signifying value that the microcosm might come to assume. The containment practiced in *The Tombs* does not, to Medina's credit, involve pulling any punches as to the dimensions of the rape of individuals necessary to subject them to the all-powerful and inescapable social dynamic. Rather, it involves the need, no matter how unrealistic—in the way in which all culture is unrealistic, because it is in the end not historical reality itself but only a (wishful) interpretation of it—to sidestep the social dynamic and to open up the possibility of contradicting it. Such containments and such attempts at contradiction are pathetically inadequate, given the structural overdetermination of the process of control through the rape of the dissenting individual. All of which means that the particular resonances of a novel like *The Tombs*, for both those sympathetic to its denunciations and those anxious to censor it as antisocial (or in perhaps a greater act of violence, to pretend it does not exist), are a function of the problematical ways in which it meshes with a social dynamic that, after all, is unimpeachably there.

CHAPTER 4

Of Power and Virgins

Alejandra Pizarnik's *La condesa sangrienta*

From a radical feminist perspective it is clear that "Father" is precisely the one who cannot exorcise, for he is allied with and identified with The Possessor. The fact that he is himself possessed should not be women's essential concern. It is a mistake to see men as pitiable victims or vessels to be "saved" through female self-sacrifice. However possessed males may be within patriarchy, it is *their* order; it is they who feed on women's stolen energy. It is a trap to imagine that women should "save" men from the dynamics of demonic possession; and to attempt this is to fall deeper into the pit of patriarchal possession. It is women ourselves who will have to expel the Father from ourselves, becoming our own exorcists.

—Mary Daly
Gyn/ecology: The Metaethics of Radical Feminism

The fundamental challenge presented by a literature of the horrible is for the reader to accept how what it is describing has anything to do with historical reality. Indeed, one of the principal cultural derivatives of the so-called Gothic component of Romanticism is the Gothic romance,[1] a product of popular culture

---

1. Kay J. Mussell, "Gothic Novels."

based on the usually hackneyed reelaboration of conventional formulas associated with the "hidden forces of the universe." One
feels safe in saying that this literature is never taken seriously
by most of its readers, for whom it is a thrilling form of escape
from the humdrum texture of the everyday social world rather
than a cultural product that allows them insights into historical
reality. The impression that the horrible is not really a truth about
the world, that it may deal with the hidden and terrible forces of
the human psyche (certainly, the thrust of the Romantic's understanding of the Gothic) but not really with the dynamics of social relations (hence, the common differentiation between romance
and novel in the Anglo-American critical tradition), leads to a
margination of the horrible. Such a margination may be performed
by readers whose tastes encourage a consumerist production of
popular writing and film production, and by critics who are neither interested in popular writing nor, beyond Romanticism, much
interested in treatments of the horrible.

In those cases in which the horrible is tied to specific sociopolitical events like the disappeared in Argentina during recent military dictatorships, the slaughter between government and guerrilla forces in El Salvador, or the massacre of indigenous tribes
in the Brazilian jungle to facilitate the construction of the Trans-
Amazonian Highway, the horrible is processed as the ugly face
of tyranny that has suddenly been revealed to decent people. The
implication, of course, is that they should repudiate it as inhuman,
as a debasement of what is naturally right. The ethics of the dis-
juncture that is thus rhetorically configured allows readers both
to confirm their own decency and to repudiate the horrible that
is being exposed to them. In this relatively circumscribed arena,
the horrible is separated from the dark recesses of the human soul
where the Romantics had discovered it and attributed to repudiated individuals, who are then seen as "amoral," "degenerate,"
and "sick."

Clearly, the extension of a binary opposition between the Good
and the Bad, between the blonde heroine and her dark-skinned
rapist, cannot do much either to restore the Romantic sense of

the horrible as a constant of human character or to go beyond the specifically sociopolitical to ground it in the structure of the historically material. To begin with, the definition of what constitutes the horrible must be (re)interpreted since it is a concept charged in terms of emotional and even psychosomatic reactions and is relative to what is judged horrible in different social and historical circumstances. Sexual taboos provide a good illustration of this: the almost universal horror inspired only a generation ago by abortion and by "the sin which dare not speak its name" is challenged by open and frank discussions of women's rights over her own body and by lesbian and gay liberation movements. It is not necessary for abortion and homosexuality to be casually accepted in American society for one to understand how the merest hint of them no longer inspires gut-wrenching revulsion in the populace. Indeed, the agenda for the moral right in both cases has had to include the essential need to revivify through artful rhetoric the lost sense of general horror these two phenomena seemed only yesterday to inspire so easily and "naturally." Yet it is not necessary to underwrite an eternal standard of the immoral in order to begin to work with a concept of the horrible grounded in specific discourse practices and the reader responses they postulate through the processes of textual implications. For example, we may no longer react in the same way to the sense of horror toward interracial sexual intercourse ascribed to readers' expectations as they are encoded in works like Faulkner's novels (where the horror of a work may turn on the discovery of such proscribed sexual activity) to understand how the work was appealing to its readership on the basis of a sense of the horrible. Conversely, we can add a sense of horror—or at least energetic repudiation— to elements now seen as sexist but which earlier readers might not have found objectionable, such as sexually enriching rapes for the woman's own good in the Mike Hammer or Norman Mailer tradition. Horror, as a metric of what is reprehensible in either moral or social terms, or in a realm of consciousness that combines the two, is founded on specific perceptions of what material reality is and on what may be perceived as a categorical threat to one's sense of well-being.

But to return to the problem of reinstalling horror in an interpretation of historical reality, it would seem that the first move must be in terms of how what is presented as horrible is in some way a dense concentration of an integral facet of human experience, and not something that is viewed as a character supplement that takes possession of only some individuals and turns them into a threat to putatively normal people. To function as a perception of the materially historical, the horrible has to be installed in the center of what is being viewed as human experience, where it will be shown to be a dominant factor in the configuration of a social reality individuals know as their world and against which they struggle for liberation. In this sense, the horrible is an index of historical necessity, and it can only have meaning in a sense beyond the gratuitously fantastic or escapist as an index of the confines of history that individuals must repudiate to avoid psychological and physical degradation. As Janice A. Radway observes about the groups of women readers she studied, "[They] are quite willing to acknowledge that the romances which so preoccupy them are little more than fantasies or fairy tales that always end happily. They readily admit in fact that the characters and events discovered in the pages of the typical romance do not resemble the people and occurrences they must deal with in their daily lives."[2]

In the case of *La condesa sangrienta* (The Bloody Countess, 1971, reissued 1976) by Alejandra Pizarnik (1936–1972), the real-life Erzébet Báthory (d. 1614), a Hungarian countess, is the focal point for a meditation on the horror of absolute power.[3] This power is expressed in sexual terms (specifically in the figure of a woman who tortures—as a form of displaced rape—and kills more than six hundred young women) whereby the ability to fulfill completely one's erotic fantasies bespeaks an absolutist social system.

Pizarnik frames her brief narrative (eleven vignettes in a sparse and highly controlled poetic prose) with two quotes that on first

---

2. Janice A. Radway, *Women Read the Romance: The Interaction of Text and Context*, 59.

3. Cf. Robert Peters, *The Blood Countess: Erzébet Bathory of Hungary*, for another fictional interpretation of the Báthory legend.

impression appear to be contradictory. The first is from Jean-Paul Sartre, who in *Saint Genet,* on the criminal/writer Jean Genet, defended the individual condemned as a criminal threat to society as in reality a privileged outsider to the structures of bourgeois repression (with his eloquent argument, Sartre literally saved Genet from execution). Pizarnik quotes Sartre as an epigraph to her text: "The criminal does not make beauty; he himself is the authentic beauty"[4] (El criminal no hace la belleza; él mismo es la auténtica belleza). After seventy pages of relentless descriptions of the sufferings inflicted on the bodies of young women placed in the countess's charge as handmaidens, Pizarnik closes with the following reflection: "Like Sade in his writings, and Gilles de Rais in his crimes, the Countess Báthory reached beyond all limits the uttermost pit of unfettered passions. She is yet another proof that the absolute freedom of the human creature is horrible" (87) (Como Sade en sus escritos, como Gilles de Rais en sus crímenes, la condesa Báthory alcanzó, más allá de todo límite, el último fondo del desenfreno. Ella es una prueba más de que la libertad absoluta de la criatura humana es horrible).

Yet these two propositions need not be viewed as contradictory. In the first place, one can assume that Sartre engaged in a deconstruction of the concept of beauty, not only in the sense of an absolute value but also as an aesthetic category divorced from a grounding in lived experience. It is possible to imagine that the thrust of this declaration is that, to the extent that the criminals are totally circumscribed by the materiality of life (both in the historical necessity that makes them criminals and in the ways in which the forces of society provide the definition of their existence and control their bodies, ultimately through incarceration), they are the most authentic indexes of the quality of our collective life and, hence, its most "beautiful" exponent. By contemplating them we can most know about ourselves, most experience the sort of transcendental self-knowledge traditionally attributed (at least

4. Pizarnik, *The Bloody Countess,* 71. All translations are from *The Bloody Countess* as translated by Alberto Manguel, and are hereafter cited parenthetically in the text.

in bourgeois aesthetics) to the beautiful that is outside our lived experience. But Sartre's object of beauty does not lead us outside the materiality of our historical circumstance and into an ineffable realm we seek to inhabit as a release from the social realm we cannot handle. Rather, it leads us squarely back into sociohistorical reality because what is being called the beautiful is exactly what is most bound (literally by the chains of the criminal, figuratively by the network of signifiers that define the criminal) by sociohistorical reality. The concept of the beautiful is now, from the perspective of Sartre's formulation, that which most brings us to an awareness of the substance of our lived social experience.

From this point of view, then, the story of Erzébet Báthory does not belong to a disjunctive realm of the abstractly beautiful, even when that beauty may be based on the systematic inversion of the primes underlying the notion of the beautiful as the ennobling— seen in these terms, Báthory would be the point-by-point refutation of the figure of woman as soul-fulfilling beauty for her masculine contemplator, something like a negative image of the Virgin Mary tradition of feminine representation. Not only is Báthory the *belle dame sans merci* inversion of the Virgin Mary sign (in the tradition of Mario Praz's "romantic agony"), but also her corporeality, which is incarnated by the horror of her sexual conduct, leads to a regrounding in historical materiality: Báthory embodies masculinist violence, the rape of the Other. In her activities as a rapist she is a symbol both of the absolute power of the aristocrats of her own historical period (she is saved from execution, despite the threats of a peasant uprising, because her family receives protection from the Hapsburg crown), and of the absolute power of the military tyranny in Argentina at the time in which *The Bloody Countess* was first read. For this reason, it would be a mistake to see Báthory as exemplifying the patriarchy's myth of feminine evil that Mary Daly has denounced in her writings: the countess's apparent crossing over the boundaries of civilization into the realm of the Wild Hag is, as I will argue in what follows, not the sort of transgression advocated by radical feminism, but is in fact a confirmation of the terrible masculinist violence of the patriarchy whose martyrs are betokened by the countess's hundreds of female victims. Báthory may have been a woman, but her relationship with the girls who came under her authority is the confirmation of the masculinist establishment she exemplified because it had created her and given her the terrible abusive power she exercised:

> Each of [the] subcultures of sadism has its own hierarchy, apprenticeship, initiation rites, and its own language. . . . Moreover, women have a special role in these subcultures as subservient token torturers of other women. The "bitch of Buchenwald" and female torturers of female political prisoners in such countries as Argentina are illustrations of this traitor-token syndrome.[5]

Pizarnik's novel became an underground classic in Argentina and is now, in its two editions, one of the rarest items in the bibliography of contemporary Argentine writing, in large measure because the historical necessity she describes for the victims of the bloody countess echoes that of the thousands of victims of the dirty war. The dirty war, waged against anything that could be accused of being leftist subversion, was confirmed as a major policy by the 1976 coup, although it was unleashed by fascistic elements in 1975 during the constitutional presidency of María Estela de Perón. Although this organized, violent elimination of dissident voices was prefigured by the human rights abuses of the dictatorships between 1966 and 1973, the period from 1976 through the end of the decade saw a quantum jump in the use of torture and political imprisonment in Argentina and the invention of the transitive verb *desaparecer* (disappeared), as described in the report of the democratic government's commission on human rights abuse, *Nunca más.*[6]

The sadomasochism Pizarnik attributes to Báthory, which is to be sure part of the legend of the Dracula genre and of the Sadean legacy of the continuum of sex and power, is a constant motif in

5. Mary Daly, *Gyn/ecology: The Metaethics of Radical Feminism*, 96.
6. Argentina, Comisión Nacional sobre la Desaparición de Personas, *Nunca más*; see also Ximena Ortúzar, *Represión y tortura en el cono sur*; *Tortura en América*; *Torture in the Eighties.*

treatments of the psychology of the torturer as *he* confronts a victim over whom he exercises complete power, particularly when that victim is a woman.[7] See, for example, the novel *Abel Rodríguez y sus hermanos* (Abel Rodríguez and His Brothers, 1981) by Ana Vásquez, a psychologist who works with victims of torture, and Eduardo Pavlovsky's play *El Sr. Galíndez* (Mr. Galíndez, 1973), in which a group of bored torturers entertain themselves with a couple of prostitutes with whom for the men sex means playfully torturing them. If the victims of Báthory are young girls, the emphasis of lesbianism added to her sadomasochism only enhances the sense of horror for her readers whose conventions are likely to lead them to find lesbianism in itself horrible enough, just as the fictional treatments and documentary reports on male torturers and their male victims may emphasize homoerotic dimensions (for example, Beatriz Guido's *El incendio y las vísperas* [The fire and the nights before it; 1963]).

It is immaterial whether "real" homosexuality is involved: one could insist that sexuality to one degree or another is involved in all human relations, and heterosexuality versus homosexuality is only a matter of calling attention to the gendered identities of the conjugation of participants of the moment.[8] Nor is it a matter of documentary reports versus fictional accounts, since one presumes that the latter bear some sort of reasonable correspondence to the former, and accounts will call attention to the distribution of the sexes between torturers and their victims. Male torturers and some kind of ratio between male and female victims are likely to be the norm, but the historical record reveals that, in the case of the bloody countess, a female torturer and more than six hundred female victims provided the basic statistics Pizarnik interprets. Rather, where sexuality enters explicitly—rhetorically—into the analysis of the confrontation between torturer and victim, it might well be because the author wishes to appeal to the sense of horror for the

7. Cf. Alicia Partnoy, *The Little School: Tales of Disappearance, Survival in Argentina,* for one woman's personal testimony.

8. See Foster, *Gay and Lesbian Themes,* 97–102; and Foster, "The Manipulation of Horizons of Reader Expectation," on the lesbian dimensions of Pizarnik's text.

presumed reader associated with the violation of certain sexual taboos: torture as sex violates one taboo (grounded in the prohibition of necrophilia, but also because torture, like rape, involves unwilling participation by one of the partners in the act), and homosexuality sharpens the horror by underscoring the transgression of yet another taboo.

What serves as the central core of Pizarnik's narrative, as it does for the narrative of the historical record she is reproducing, is the series of clashes between the powerful and the unprotected, the authoritarian figure and her protégées (in the case of the military dictatorship in Argentina, it is the state versus its citizens), absolute freedom and historical necessity. The countess—like any one of the figures of despotism she personifies—occupies a position from which she can dictate in an absolute manner the rules of society, and it is a dictatorship from which her victims can have no appeal or escape: they are absolutely circumscribed by the jail of the text she has forged. This relationship is cameoed in the vignette "La jaula mortal" (The lethal cage):

> Lined with knives and adorned with sharp iron blades, it can hold one human body, and can be lifted by means of a pulley. The ceremony of the cage takes place in this manner:
>
> Dorko the maid drags in by the hair a naked young girl, shuts her up in the cage and lifts it high into the air. The Lady of These Ruins appears, a sleepwalker in white. Slowly and silently she sits upon a footstool placed underneath the contraption.
>
> A red-hot poker in her hand, Dorko taunts the prisoner who, drawing back (and this is the ingenuity of the cage) stabs herself against the sharp irons while her blood falls upon the pale woman who dispassionately receives it, her eyes fixed on nothing, as in a daze. When the lady recovers from the trance, she slowly leaves the room. There have been two transformations: her white dress is now red, and where a girl once stood a corpse now lies. (73)
>
> (Tapizada con cuchillos y adornada con filosas puntas de acero, su tamaño admite un cuerpo humano; se la iza mediante una polea. La ceremonia de la jaula se despliega así:

La sirvienta Dorkó arrastra por los cabellos a una joven des-
nuda; la encierra en la jaula; alza la jaula. Aparece la "dama de
estas ruinas", la sonámbula vestida de blanco. Lenta y silenciosa
se sienta en un escabel situado debajo de la jaula.

Rojo atizador en mano, Dorkó azuza a la prisionera quien,
al retroceder —y he aquí la gracia de la jaula—, se clava por sí
misma los filosos aceros mientras su sangre mana sobre la mujer
pálida que la recibe impasible con los ojos puestos en ningún lado.
Cuando se repone de su trance se aleja lentamente. Han habido
dos metamorfosis: su vestido blanco ahora es rojo y donde hubo
una muchacha hay un cadáver.)

Pizarnik's writing is almost a parody of Parnassian prose, in the
sense of creating a visual sculpture in the fashion of Mallarmé's
"Art poétique." The curious use of words such as *lined* and *ingenuity* contribute to the sense of aesthetic distancing, duplicated
by the entranced detachment of the spectator countess, the "Lady
of These Ruins." She contemplates the literal figure of her power,
the cage in which the victim is imprisoned, just as the citizens of
her realm are caged by the absolute power she wields over them.
Caught between Dorko's red-hot poker and the spikes of the cage,
the victim dies by being driven against the hard-edged reality of
the cage. The double transformation described at the end of the
vignette is a process of confirmation of the countess's horrifying,
vampirical power: the transference to her of the blood of the girl
nullifies the victim while invigorating the owner of the cage (the
text speaks elsewhere of elements of witchcraft in Báthory's use of
the blood of her victims to maintain her youth and beauty; one of
the vignettes is entitled "Baños de sangre" [Bloodbaths]).

It is interesting to note that in these vignettes the narrator uses
the present tense. Less than a remote historical event, what she
is recounting is, to use a grammatical term, a durative present,
an existing reality that is in a sense tenseless, much like the use
of the present in mathematical formulas or scientific propositions.
Báthory bespeaks the inherent coordinates of the exercise of violent
power, a dynamic of horrifying oppression in which she is only a
transitory agent but which she inherits and which will exist after

her, as the Argentine dirty war and regrettably so many other historical circumstances have confirmed. Certainly, it is customary for poetry—and the texts of *The Bloody Countess*, Pizarnik's only prose composition, are in reality prose poems—to be written in the durative present, to the extent that we associate with poetry the specification of "eternal truths" rather than the time-bound accounts of prose fiction. But the eternal truth of *The Bloody Countess* is to be read as unquestionably sociohistorically grounded not because of the historical figure of Báthory, but because of the dynamic of power she exemplifies.

The irony of Pizarnik's sculptured prose, however, is that the beauty of the countess lies not in the images of her physical attributes, the ingeniousness of her handling of the landscape she controls, or the power of the symbols of her dramatic tableaux (for example, the interplay between deathly white and enlivening blood red). Rather it lies in the economy of her horrible incarnation of the criminal whose acts are shown to lead us back into a historical materiality that imprisons us all. The lurid fascination of a narrative such as *The Bloody Countess* can only be the contemplation of a reality that we experience in our daily lives, perhaps less vividly but at times in all of its literalness (such as with the dirty war). In this experience we are confronted with the violent abusiveness of a sociopolitical system that we have not yet been able to change, a murderous cage that we have not yet been able to escape from. And the text's reference to how the girl is obliged to impale herself on the spikes of the cage, as though she were responsible for her own pain and death, is a token of how we are not just victims of a system that oppresses us but also its perpetuators and (re)inventors in the betrayal of the self. The passiveness of Báthory's victims, their inability to find a form of revolt, makes them accomplices in their own suffering until the threat of a peasants' revolt (the majority of Báthory's victims were peasant girls, although some noblewomen placed in her charge were involved) puts an end to the countess's highly efficient enactments of the larger structure of oppression.

Pizarnik's text turns on the motif of contemplation, of sexual voyeurism. Báthory contemplates the drama of suffering enacted for her by her servants and her victims (although she does, on occasion, handle the instruments of torture herself), and, of course, the reader contemplates Báthory's role as a spectator and, through her, the representation of absolute power. The vignette "La virgen de hierro" (The iron maiden) is only one of the texts that centers on voyeurism and the reduplication of the countess in the object of the iron maiden serves to underscore the displacement between the countess and the instruments of her power that she—and through her, the reader—contemplates:

> There was once in Nuremberg a famous automaton known as the Iron Maiden. The Countess Báthory bought a copy for her torture chamber in Csejthe Castle. This clockwork doll was of the size and colour of a human creature. Naked, painted, covered in jewels, with blond hair that reached down to the ground, it had a mechanical device that allowed it to curve its lips into a smile, and to move its eyes.
> The Countess, sitting on her throne, watches.
> For the Maiden to spring into action it is necessary to touch some of the precious stones in its necklace. It responds immediately with horrible creaking sounds and very slowly lifts its white arms which close in a perfect embrace around whatever happens to be next to it—in this case, a girl. The automaton holds her in its arms and now no one will be able to uncouple the living body from the body of iron, both equally beautiful. Suddenly the painted breasts of the Iron Maiden open, and five daggers appear that pierce her struggling companion whose hair is as long as its own.
> Once the sacrifice is over another stone in the necklace is touched: the arms drop, the smile and the eyes fall shut, and the murderess becomes once again the Maiden, motionless in its coffin. (71–72)

> (Había en Nuremberg un famoso autómata llamado "la Virgen de hierro". La condesa Báthory adquirió una réplica para la sala de torturas de su castillo de Csejthe. Esta dama metálica era del tamaño y del color de la criatura humana. Desnuda, maquillada, enjoyada, con rubios cabellos que llegaban al suelo, un mecanismo permitía que sus labios se abrieran en una sonrisa, que los ojos se movieran.

La condesa, sentada en su trono, contempla.

Para que la "Virgen" entre en acción es preciso tocar algunas piedras preciosas de su collar. Responde inmediatamente con horrible sonidos mecánicos y muy lentamente alza los blancos brazos para que se cierren en perfecto abrazo sobre lo que esté cerca de ella—en este caso una muchacha. La autómata la abraza y ya nadie podrá desanudar el cuerpo vivo del cuerpo de hierro, ambos iguales en belleza. De pronto se abren y aparecen cinco puñales que atraviesan a su viviente compañera de largos cabellos sueltos como los suyos.

Ya consumado el sacrificio, se toca otra piedra del collar: los brazos caen, la sonrisa se cierra así como los ojos, la asesina vuelva a ser la "Virgen" inmóvil en su féretro.)

Voyeurism is also a sexual taboo, although perhaps not as strongly repudiated as necrophilia, rape, and homosexuality. One suspects we all allow ourselves an indulgence in voyeurism if we think we are not ourselves being watched engaged in the act of watching—the *Rear Window* syndrome. Reading, which is paradigmatically a solitary vice, is a form of voyeurism—we contemplate a world that we are not likely to otherwise have access to. Such voyeurism, with or without reference to sexuality, may be encoded metanarratively in the text or it may remain only a part of the reader's (un)conscious sense of invading the space of the Other being read about. An excellent example is Julio Cortázar's short story "Las babas del diablo" ("Blow-up"), in which the reader voyeuristically watches the agony of the photographer-voyeur as he contemplates, in the photograph he has taken and now away from a real-life situation in which he cannot intervene, the horror of a boy being doubly seduced by a man and his female accomplice. In Pizarnik's text, in addition to the explicit homosexuality of the act of voyeurism on the part of the countess, a challenge is made to the gaze of the reader, who (through the eyes of the narrator, who is the mediating voyeur) watches the countess watch herself embracing her victim through the agency of the iron maiden. It is the horror of what the voyeur sees, compounded by the violation of the taboo of voyeurism, that undoubtedly is the basis of repugnance many readers experience in the face of a text like *The*

Bloody Countess. Yet it is this horror that must also be the basis of a reentry, through the literary text, into the reality of the social text and a perception of how the horror of the former, the product of the artful distillation of the resources of the artist's craft, is a figure of the horrors of the actual oppression of abusive power that permeates, albeit often in a diluted form, everyday historical reality. If voyeurs are often spellbound by what they see, it is because the scene evokes a perceived logic of human relations, and if what is witnessed is felt to be horrible, that horror is not an independent aesthetic judgment but rather a reliable index of what we sense to be horrible in the world we are condemned inescapably to inhabit.

We need now to reconcile the figure of Báthory as a criminal both as she is constructed by her society and as she is a mirror of it (one of the vignettes, entitled "El espejo de la melancolía" ["The melancholy mirror"], adds a series of mirror metaphors to the subject of self-contemplation). Báthory, like every human being, is heir to the social code of her society. All individuals are instruments for the articulation of a social ideology, and the horizons of self-consciousness are basically defined by the code internalized as part of the process of socialization. For this reason, someone like Báthory cannot be conceived of as a "monster" that exists outside the structure of her society, and precisely the ideological slippage found in much literature of the horror and documentary reports on so-called monsters is to construe them as existing outside the structures of what is smugly called the "normal" world: the "abnormal" world of the pervert exists somewhere else, although its citizens will on occasion invade the world of the decent when its defenses are carelessly lowered. But I have suggested that the sense of the Sartre quote is to view the criminal as the vivid encoding of the degrading principles of human commerce that circulate relatively unchecked in society: the criminal is the paradigm of all men and the persecution of the criminal derives from the threat of the eloquence with which criminality represents how the real world is. The bloody countess is, therefore, a circumstantial embodiment, but a very dramatic one, of the abusive power permitted to certain individuals in her age.

It is significant to note that, because of the loyalties sustaining the Hapsburg Empire, Erzébet Báthory was not executed for her amply documented crimes—just as the agents of the dirty war in Argentina and of similar operations in other Latin American countries went essentially unpunished for their crimes (top military officials in Argentina sentenced to prison by courts during the Alfonsín government were nevertheless pardoned by Menem, his successor, in 1989). Báthory was immured in her castle, and her imprisonment, a replicated sign of the torture chamber of her victims, lasted three years until her death in 1614: "She never understood why she had been condemned" (86) (Nunca comprendió por qué la condenaron). Criminals often do not understand what their relationship is to the system that has engendered them and then condemned them for what they embody, and Báthory (like the *generales* who to this day protest their innocence and insist that the country owes them a monument for their deeds on behalf of the Fatherland) remained unaware of the system of power relations of her society that her sexual dramatics so efficiently enacted. Those power relations were to be given full representation on the broad stage of life during the Thirty Years War, one of the bloodiest conflicts of premodern European history, in which the Hapsburgs were involved between 1618 and 1648. The causes leading up to the war made the Hapsburg crown especially concerned about bonds of loyalty that involved Báthory's family.

One of the problems with a literature of the horrible is the chance that the horrors it portrays will become naturalized or that it is only possible because they are, in fact, already acceptable: motifs from *Halloween, Friday the Thirteenth, Carrie, The Exorcist,* and *The Texas Chainsaw Massacre* have become motifs in contemporary American pop culture to be repeated (through numerous sequels) and reelaborated (through numerous spinoffs). Naturalization here means that they become accepted as continuous with what is recognized unreflexively as expected in the cultural paradigm. As such they lose their shock value as being monstrous or horrible, perhaps retaining only the disembodied aesthetic thrill of the conventionally horrible. There is an inherent contradiction here, of course. One does want to argue for the incorporation of the horrible within an understanding of what is possible in the dynamics of quotidian reality: torture, rape, and calculatedly sadistic murder are of a whole with the parameters of the ideology that sustains the intercourse of known human experience, the historical materialism to which one constantly refers as the imperative grounding for cultural texts and analyses of them.[9] But in the process of seeing someone like Báthory as the extreme embodiment of what we accept as the natural exercise of sociopolitical power, we cannot allow room for seeing her conduct as natural, as no longer inspiring horror or revulsion, in the realm of what we think our society to be or what we want it to be, which is the danger of seeing the bloody countess as beautiful in terms of the bourgeois concept of an ideal, otherworldly beauty. The Sartre quote, it has been argued, separates itself from this notion of beauty, and Pizarnik is careful to enunciate at the end of her text a position that retains the bloody countess as a figure very much of this world, but precisely therefore not one deserving of either our sympathy or our emulation:

> She was never afraid, she never trembled. And no compassion, no sympathy may be felt for her. Only a certain astonishment at the enormity of the horror, a fascination with a white dress that turns red, with the idea of total laceration, with the imagination of a silence starred with cries in which everything reflects an unacceptable beauty. (86–87)

> (Ella no sintió miedo, no tembló nunca. Entonces, ninguna compasión ni emoción ni admiración por ella. Sólo un quedar en suspenso en el exceso de horror, una fascinación por un vestido blanco que se vuelve rojo, por la idea de un absoluto desgarramiento, por la evocación de un silencio constelado de gritos en donde todo es la imagen de una belleza inaceptable.)

As a consequence, our sense of the horror of the world as represented by *The Bloody Countess* can only be a metric of our perception of the dynamics of abusive power that sustain the world

9. Cf. Jean Franco, "Gender, Death and Resistance: Facing the Ethical Vacuum."

we actually live in. This more than anything else explains the enormous importance that Pizarnik's text on a forgotten Hungarian countess of almost four hundred years ago, yet written at a dreadful time in recent Argentine history, has had among those struggling to understand the nature of their own immediate world.

Yet there is an important distinction to be made between the image of the exercise of violence that Pizarnik portrays in terms of Erzébet Báthory and the documented human rights abuses of the military regimes under which many of the Argentine readers of *The Bloody Countess* were formed. As appalling as the use of torture and murder by the military was, it served a putatively practical purpose: the consolidation of political power whereby the use of violence would serve to stifle opposition to the dictatorship. By contrast, the already consolidated power that Báthory wielded from within the absolutist confines of her castle could have had no other purpose than to allay the tedium of her melancholy. Although there are some references to blood rituals meant to preserve her youth and beauty, only some of the practices she engaged in were meant for that purpose. In the main, her activities had no more goal than the aesthetic display of the ingenuity of violence. While some of the agents of military repression may have been engaged in fulfilling personal needs akin to those of the countess, the apparatus as such served a very pragmatic function absent in the universe Pizarnik describes.

Finally, we must return to the matter of Báthory as a figure of masculinist violence. It is cruelly ironic that *The Bloody Countess* involves a woman exercising such power over other women, and she may be viewed as an example of what Daly has called the female "token torturer," the woman who is an agent of the sado-rituals men practice on the bodies of women. But like Dante's Perillo (*Inferno*, 27), Báthory becomes a victim of the masculinist power she embodies, as she is, in turn, sacrificed by the structure of oppression she has personified for her victims. When it becomes politically expedient to punish her for her crimes, crimes made possible by the power invested in the criminal, she is condemned to immurement, which in its own way is a grim figure of "la jaula mortal."

CHAPTER 5

Disappearing Argentina

Marta Lynch's *Informe bajo llave*

F ar-fetchedness, perhaps, may be the only way of dealing with historical phenomena such as the Argentine holocaust. Undoubtedly, there is a significant utilitarianism in texts of a documentary or testimonial nature, and there has certainly been an impressive spate of these: the centerpiece is, without a question, *Nunca más* (Never more, 1984), the Report of the Commission on the Disappeared, the catalog and chronicle commissioned by the president that marks the definitive official confirmation of that holocaust. To be sure, this work and other translated texts, such as Joan Didion's *Salvador*, have abetted, in a ghoulish sort of way, the self-congratulatory perceptions of the First World about the "incivility of life in the Third World." Such texts run the very real risk of promoting an attitude of resignation toward the abridgement of human rights in Latin America, to the effect that the problem is so staggering that "nothing can really be done." The result of this gesture, at least as far as literary works may be concerned, is a distancing of the reader beyond the pale of any sense of responsibility for the sociohistorical reality being contemplated. I am convinced that this is the case with recent works published in English on the period of repression in Argentina.[1]

1. For more on testimonial texts, see Foster, "Narrativa testimonial argentina durante los años del 'Proceso.'" In addition to *Nunca más,* see also R. Dworkin's introduction to the English translation. For more on the distancing effect of some documentary texts, see Foster, "Imagining Argentine Socio-Political History." The

115

By far-fetchedness, one does not mean to gather up the various forms of allegorical writing—quasi, pseudo, or neo—that some critical opinion has discerned as one type of response to general social repression and the specific cultural repression of censorship and intimidation. To the degree that things that must be said cannot be said directly, writing that is overtly allegorical (because it is markedly disengaged from documentary coordinates) is alleged to emerge as a sort of scriptive pact between writers and their readers, who presumably are thirsty enough for versions of their infernal life that they will undertake the often tedious task of transcoding allegory back into history.[2] Whether the allegories are expressed in terms of a national setting placed on the other side of the looking glass of documentary or in terms of a foreign (often otherworldly) setting that is "safe" because it does not immediately conform to the contours of the politically knowable, they offer the opportunity to plumb the wrenching violence of historical circumstance via a cultural text that, in fact, cannot say that it is dealing with that circumstance. The cost in terms of attributing the actual stuff of the text, the sociohistorical dimensions of the characters and their acts, to a radically absurdist conception of history, to a realm of the fantastic where lived events cannot be linked to a real plan of human business, is proportional to the extent to which the allegorical code successfully masks its semantic bases in the specific historical reality. This is often undertaken in the first instance as a strategy for fending off censorship and other inconvenient oppressions.

This sort of allegorical writing has unquestionably been important in Argentina and elsewhere in Latin America not only as an antiphony to the staggering degradation of public cultural discourse during times of tyranny, but as quite simply a way to continue against the backdrop of the draconian attempts to contain

novels examined are Jay Cantor, *The Death of Che Guevara* (1983); Douglas Mine, *Champions of the World* (1988); Lawrence Thornton, *Imagining Argentina* (1987); and Douglas Unger, *El Yanqui* (1986).

2. Bronislava Volek and Emil Volek, "*Guinea Pigs* and the Czech Novel 'Under Padlock.'"

and tame the threat of cultural production.[3] Like all markedly allegorical writing (and setting aside the obvious: all expression is "allegorical," to the extent that it is based on transcoding reality that can only come forth as already semiotically configured and not simply as itself as such), these texts both allow a measure of access to an interpretive rewriting of the sociopolitical text and defer the latter by virtue of the internal coherence of the otherworldly and not immediately historically referential narrative. Aside from the possibilities of writers thereby protecting themselves from censorship by not being aggressively literal, an allegorical discourse that opens up the sign system by connecting the semantic primes of contemporary historical experience with a broader panorama of human events intersect with a mode of expression that encourages a slippage of contemporary historical experience toward, if not its outright displacement in favor of, a contrary or alternate realm of social experience whose links with the reader's lived experience become radically attenuated.

A discourse of far-fetchedness accomplishes something quite different. The overall pattern of references in the text coordinate to a high degree of predictability with the outlines of what can be called acknowledged or documented facts: events are reported that correspond to what readers already (think they) know about contemporary historical experience, while the reported actors may be known figures so thinly disguised that the disguise itself is annoyingly coy. The network of relations between actors and events *in general* matches a norm of verisimilitude that confirms our society's expectations that writers, readers, and fictional texts are engaged in a process representing sociohistorical reality in a recognizable way, no matter how much that representation may be densely cast within the various modernist and postmodernist conventions of contemporary narrative, which may, of course, include the option of one or another variety of allegorical transcodification.

Where a narrative may veer off into what is here being loosely called far-fetchedness is in the introduction of a plot loop that,

3. Avellaneda, *Censura, autoritarismo y cultura.*

within the confines of the close adherence to perceived sociohistorical realities and backed up with varying degrees of implied or
direct documentary evidence (for example, the mixed-media techniques of incorporating newspaper clippings, public declarations,
intertextual excursuses and the like) is a projection of events and
actors toward configurations that are not quite as easily correlat-
able with a presumed norm of accepted, "realistic" facts. Such an
extrapolation is, however, double-edged. In the first instance, it
may imply a calculus of historical interpretation whereby what is
apparently far-fetched can be demonstrated to be in some way a
reasonable consequence of circumstances within the purview of the
norm of acknowledgeable facts. Given some particular historical
circumstance, what seems outlandish may be shown to be a possible evolution of the facts: if it is only realistic to admit that, today,
doctors and lawyers may be sued for malpractice, it cannot, upon
close reflection, be far-fetched to suggest that the day will come
when professors can just as easily be held liable for the malpractice
of their profession. On a somewhat more relevant sociohistorical
level, the American retrograde trajectory of law and order may,
to alleviate the prison overcrowding it has spawned, lead to a
return to a more extensive application of the death penalty, as
some citizens earnestly advocate.

In a second instance, the departure from facts that are felt to be
verifiable may serve to alert the reader to private knowledge that
lies outside the domain of what is verifiable. American culture is
particularly susceptible to writing that makes the claim to have
access to a "secret dossier" of information, information that will
open up to readers a hidden (in both the passive and the active
sense of the word) domain of comings and goings that will convince them that everyday surface reality and the customary reports
about it are either distractions from the real truth or only its barest
outlines. Satisfying a deep-seated paranoia that "they" are keeping
something from us—and, undoubtedly, it is a paranoia fed by just
enough manipulation of the facts to make it plausible; take, for
example, the enormous gaps between what the CIA has claimed
to be doing at any one time and subsequent reconstructions of

what was really involved—such writing provides a range of cultural texts that supplement what the sociopolitical establishment sustains as historical reality. That this paranoia is a well-entrenched component of the popular culture of American society is confirmed by the productive refashionings of its conventions undertaken by high-culture writers like Kurt Vonnegut or Thomas Pynchon, although there can be little question that Joseph Heller's *Catch-22* (1961) is the paradigmatic example.

In the case of Latin America, the appeal to an unreported and supposedly richer concealed reality makes more sense because of the greater onslaughts the Western ideal of freedom of the press has endured there. The result has been the tradition of documentary narratives like those of Rodolfo Walsh, whose success in probing official lies probably is what led him to become one of the most prominent writers among Argentina's disappeared persons after the 1976 military coup. Yet the attempt to painstakingly reconstruct some *plausible* sense of what happened is, in reality, a check on the far-fetchedness of official explanations, whereby the extravagance of the proposed truth, by virtue of the sheer weight of the evidence involved in conformance with accepted public knowledge over how the machine of repression and oppression works, serves to cancel out official explanations, which then become the far-fetched narrative fictions of self-serving tyrants. Thus, for example, the Argentine military's argument that its involvement in the wholesale slaughter of the citizenry was a far-fetched lie, one that was patently unreasonable, had necessarily to yield to the nightmarish truth of the documentary evidence carefully amassed by the National Commission on Disappeared Persons, whereby the far-fetched was proved to be historical reality.

This sort of semiotic operation, involving the inversion of the binary opposition of far-fetched versus documentary, is clearly a significant component of cultural texts in Latin American societies where a contestatorial narrative production is carried out within the context of official versions of historical reality that many citizens are not willing to accept as being truthful. To the extent that the American public is willing to accept the versions provided by its official and professional press, such alternate versions, *National Enquirer*–style, are confined to the realm of popular culture and consumed in the main as cheaply delightful or titillating tales whose very far-fetchedness renders them harmless, albeit exasperating to the guardians of journalistic or literary professionalism who view them as a defiance of the professions' earnest seriousness.

Clearly, then, something else must be involved in the role of far-fetchedness as a narrative prime. Rather than seeing it as a reversible term in the interplay between official lies and documentary truth, as sketched above, I propose that, at least in a certain group of contemporary Latin American writings, it be seen as a strategy for highlighting a specific historical reality, sort of a way for providing greater depth to a narrative formulation that has, perhaps, become automatized as regards its social and historical meanings: the amplification of its complex meanings, shading off into the far-fetched (again, at least in terms of some vaguely defined norm), regrounds the particular narreme as of special significance within the literary reconstruction of the social text. For example, the dramatic accumulation of rape scenes, typically criticized as rhetorically excessive because it is alleged to be statistically exaggerated, in Enrique Medina's *The Tombs* has the function of reaffirming the way in which the prison system involves a generalized rape of individuals in all orders of their being because it is nothing more than a structured reduplication of violence to which the individual is subjected in a society built on alienation, dehumanization, and exploitation:

> Therefore, women feel the fuck—when it works, when it overwhelms—as possession; and feel possession as deeply erotic; and value annihilation of the self in sex as proof of the man's desire or love, its awesome intensity. And therefore, being possessed is phenomenologically real for women; and sex itself is an experience of diminishing self-possession, and erosion of self. That loss of self is a physical reality, not just a psychic vampirism; and as a physical reality it is chilling and extreme, a literal erosion of the body's integrity and its ability to function and to survive. The physical

rigors of sexual possession—of being possessed—overwhelm the body's vitality . . . and she, possessed, becomes weak, depleted, usurped in all her physical and mental energies and capacities by the one who has physically taken her over; by the one who occupies her. This sexual possession is a sensual state of being that borders on antibeing until it ends in death.[4]

That society "rapes" the individual and that prisons are microcosms of society is a virtual cliché, which is why literature constructed around this postulate is content to remind us with one key scene of violence; the dramatic accumulation of violence in Medina's novel is an unrelenting regrounding of this truth in a way that keeps the reader from ever forgetting it, from ever displacing it by hypocritical appeals (such as one might find even in social realism) to some ameliorating "goodness" beyond the unimpeachable and naked social fact.

Much of what is called neogrotesque writing in Argentina, particularly in the theater, involves this form of far-fetchedness: basic sociological or documentary configurations have accrued to them certain projections of character and action that segue into the realm of the far-fetched because their artistic eloquence derives, precisely, from their transgression of the perceived norm of verisimilitude. Such transgressions do not intend to entertain because they are outlandish exaggerations or wild fabrications (although many of them, in fact, do involve a sort of unusually perverse black humor), but rather pretend to be emphatic regroundings of specific sociohistoric coordinates as part of a project to represent the dynamics of the dystopian society. Thus, in Roberto Cossa's 1978 neogrotesque drama *La nona* (Grandma), the voracious, cockroachlike immigrant grandmother literally eats her family into ruin as a complex conceit whereby the immigrant's dream to make it in America to such a degree so as to always be able to eat abundantly at will is correlated with the unrelenting rapaciousness of killer-shark capitalism.[5] While superficially hilarious,

4. Dworkin, 67. Cf. also Brownmiller, *Against Our Will.*
5. Previdi Froelich, "América deshecha."

the far-fetched grotesqueries of *Grandma* serve to confirm a social reality that is all too painfully concrete and real: the central character may be an exaggeration, but the historical truth to which she points is not, and the grotesque texture of the drama prevents any slippage of the representation of that truth into sentimental hedges about tough yet lovable senior citizens that would vitiate its impact.

Perhaps one of the most significant examples of a narrative employment conforming to this concept of the far-fetched is Marta Lynch's *Informe bajo llave* (Report under lock and key, 1983), her last major novel before her suicide in 1986. Like Lynch's novels in general, *Report under Lock and Key* focuses on a woman who lives an agonizing relationship with her surroundings. Essentially considered a feminist, Lynch made use of the existential figure of the lonely individual adrift in an alienated society (and it must be remembered that contemporary Argentine fiction was particularly receptive to existential formulas) to explore the anomie of upper-middle-class women who, less than experiencing overt sexual oppression, live out the futility of a social system that basically has no use for them beyond a few rigidly defined roles. Typically, the possibility is not even contemplated that the women would derive anguish from these claustrophobic roles, as Lynch demonstrates so eloquently in *La Señora Ordóñez* (Mrs. Ordóñez, 1967), a novel that opens with a scandalous meditation on sexual frustration. In her last fiction, Lynch was able to tie her nuclear feminist concerns to even larger issues of political oppression, whereby the anguish of her characters, their sense of frustration, loss, and degradation, is viewed as the consequence of a continuum of social and political structures whose dehumanizing features are given their apotheosic embodiment in the brutal aggressions of recent military dictatorships, particularly the self-styled Proceso. In *La penúltima versión de la Colorada Villanueva* (The penultimate version of Colorada Villanueva, 1978), Lynch presents a woman who has arrived at the penultimate stage in the collapse of her personal identity as the consequence of the accumulated onslaughts of a society whose dynamic bears no coherent relationship to its abiding myths.[6]

In the case of *The Penultimate Version*, the protagonist is a sober housewife married to a university professor, although she is also engaged in running a nursery school, a respectable enough occupation for a woman of her class. In *Report under Lock and Key*, the protagonist conforms more to the superficial image of a dislocated, existential heroine. Adela is a writer whose personal problems are acute enough for her to be in analysis (the prevalence of psychological and psychiatric analysis among certain classes in Buenos Aires has the dimensions of a national trait, which is examined savagely by Alicia Steimberg in her 1987 novel, *El árbol del placer* [The tree of pleasure]). Where the novel is of exceptional interest is in the dimension of one of her personal problems.

Adela enters into a complex and ultimately destructive relationship with a man named Vargas, to all appearances a highly placed executive with ties to the military junta, during the period of the military dictatorships; the ambiguity of his exact position in Argentine finances and the military-industrial complex is undoubtedly a correlative of the shadowy nature of so many such men during the tyranny. Rather like a modern Scheherazade, she uses her literary talents to define the parameters of their relationship, and it appears that the executive's attraction to her is due to her status as a writer. While Adela may not tell Vargas stories to save herself from death, her personality as a creative force seems to be what sustains the executive's interest in her, since he is otherwise dedicated to the "dirty war" (the military's own term) of national reconstruction through the unrelenting elimination of any opposition to its activities.

The crux of the novel, however, is the never spoken question of what possible interest Adela could have in the executive, and it is here that Lynch uses an element of far-fetchedness in her novel.

6. David William Foster, "Marta Lynch: The Individual and the Argentine Political Process"; Diane S. Birkmoe, "The Virile Voice of Marta Lynch."

The text opens with a brief prologue signed by Lynch, in which she claims to have obtained Adela's chronicle of her relationship with Vargas from the former's psychoanalyst.[7] It is significant that this explanatory note does not even mention the most salient characteristic of Adela's papers, the description of her tormented and turbulent relationship with the executive. What is far-fetched about this relationship is both its very existence and what seems to have kept it going. It is, by any criterion of verisimilitude, difficult to believe that a man in the executive's position, especially during a period in which the military high command is occupied with exercising dictatorial power, would take up with someone like Adela or even have contact with any writer at all, much less a woman characterized by existential hang-ups. Of course, it is not that a full-fledged macho like Vargas would not have a lover. Indeed, it would be assumed and even expected that he would, and that he would keep her and display her in the fashion to which his sort are accustomed. But it is quite difficult to believe that sexual escapades for Vargas would mean someone like Adela and that their trysts would take place in his suite of offices rather than the time-honored *bulín* (love nest) or, as is more common nowadays, in a luxury hotel. Yet *Report under Lock and Key* assumes such a circumstance to occur, and I will return to its semiotic implications.[8]

Certainly, one immediately evident implication of this arrangement, from the point of view of the world in which Vargas lives, is the far-sweeping power that he exercises. It is a power that overflows every corner of society, enfolding within its embrace the most disparate elements, in order to meld them to its own exercise of absolute authority. Literally, Vargas embraces Adela, and his embrace is a message to her, as the index in the novel of the sort of creative force we associate with literature, that she, too, as his lover and along with her creations, is subject to his authority and

---

7. Lynch, *Informe bajo llave,* 9, hereafter cited parenthetically in the text.
8. See Alessandra Riccio, "Eros y poder en *Informe bajo llave* de Marta Lynch," for another interpretation of the relationship between sex and power in Lynch's novel.

legitimation.[9] When she also becomes one of the disappeared at the end of the novel, she has necessarily discovered that such authority includes the power to annihilate her and the inconvenience her writing now represents.

In fact, the members of the ruling junta in any military government do not exercise such all-encompassing authority. In addition to competing among themselves for supremacy (the reason for internal shifts of power and leadership during most such regimes), it has been customary for the actors in Argentine military dictatorships to divide the sectors of society up among themselves and for any one commander to guard jealously any attempt to usurp control over his prisoners and field of operations, including those whom he may, for the moment, choose to protect. While it is consonant with such a mechanics of power for the executive to both shield and destroy Adela in this fashion, as a model for the structure of tyrannical military power, its economy is weakened by the fact that the executive cannot be a simple sign for the absolute exercise of the power of life and death over an individual, since he too is a component in an exponentially greater formula of the struggle for power. Osvaldo Soriano's novel *No habrá más penas ni olvido* (A Funny, Dirty Little War, 1980) is a comic parody of this circumstance, made all the more grotesque because of the dreadful historical facts on which it is based, and Humberto Costantini's *De dioses, hombrecitos y policías* (The Gods, the Little Guys, and the Police, 1979) articulates the horrendous arbitrariness that attends to the incoherences that result from the overarching power struggles among tyrants and agents.

The reader may thus wonder about the deviation from the norm inherent in Vargas's choice of a neurotic writer like Adela for the exercises of his supermacho prerogatives, and there are questions to be raised about the totalizing power of Vargas as an exaggerated sign for military tyranny in Argentina (which is not the sort of

9. See Guido Mantega, "Sexo e poder nas sociedades autoritárias: a face erótica da dominação"; Aguinaldo Silva, "Violação: ato sexual ou de poder," on the continuities between sex and authoritarian power.

banana republic like the Guatemala of Miguel Angel Asturias's *El señor presidente* [The president, 1946], which allows the president to be viewed as one spider from which all the threads of the web emanate). Yet what is crucially far-fetched in the novel is not the executive's relationship vis-à-vis Adela, but Adela's relationship vis-à-vis him. Adela transcribes, in response to probings from her psychiatrist, a description of what it was like to make love to him. A series of preparatory acts, including eating and drinking with appropriate ceremony, culminate with the succinct "My love, I am used to using violence" (Mi amor, estoy acostumbrado a violentar, 214). This description is almost ludicrous in its carica-ture of the beauty and the beast, the latter a clumsy glutton who gorges at table and reveals the deficiencies of his upbringing (both in the lack of familiarity with the rituals of eating and the lack of subsequent training, despite his rank). Moreover, the need to preface lovemaking with hearty eating and drinking betrays an adherence to bourgeois values (the society that low-born military men aspire to emulate, we are to understand) that may be enough of an automatized index to enable Adela, her addressee, and the reader to repudiate him without compunction. Vargas is an oaf, and with this his parameters as a human being are handily described for the purposes of the novel. When, with no apparent thought for the implications of his declaration, he subsequently informs Adela that he is used to proceeding violently, oaf and rapist join hands in a figure that will need no further elaboration to establish his semantic value in the novel.

But, then, what is his attraction for Adela? Herein lies the point about *Report under Lock and Key* being far-fetched. One is struck by how Adela describes the executive's declaration of a preference for violence with the adverb "unfortunately." Most readers, with virtually no hesitation, characterize violence as something much more than "unfortunate," especially when its agent is disposed to confess so blithely to a predilection for it. Since the Proceso and its dirty war were built on an ideology that legitimated the oxymora of justified repression, necessary violence, and legal unconstitu-tionality (see Duhalde's *The Argentine Terrorist State*), it is easy to understand why the executive can make his unrestricted declaration with shameless impunity; but it is not easy to understand why Adela is satisfied with qualifying it as only unfortunate. Additionally, one need hardly stress the dimensions of rape involved with this declaration as made by an individual to a sexual partner.

Contemporary feminism has worked mightily to raise consciousness about rape as the ultimate violent sexual indignity, whether practiced against women or practiced against men and regardless of the sex of the agent. Indeed, the point made repeatedly is that while rape involves a sexual act, it is in fact an unqualified form of violence that violates the individual's most intimate sense of dignity and control over her or his body, and it is immaterial whether that sense of dignity is a natural or a cultural construct. Only murder (which often accompanies rape as an orgasmic coda; see Pedro Almodóvar's film *Matador* and its several versions of this scenario) can be viewed as a greater indignity than rape. Moreover, an integral part of the process of honing the definition of rape and of redefining its legal and social role (the former in terms of ensuring that it is prosecuted and punished and the latter in terms of demonstrating how it has served historically as a form of intimidation and degradation of women especially, but not exclusively) has been to challenge the abiding myth that there are sexual partners who prefer a form of rape, if only as an erotic game, as sexual theatrics, or as a part of sex. While it may be reasonable to maintain that there is an important distinction to be made between nonconsenting sexual violence by an agent legally to be defined as a rapist and sexual theatrics involving consenting and mutually satisfying varieties of sadomasochism (John Rechy explores some of these dimensions in his documentary *The Sexual Outlaw* [1977] and in his antisadomasochism novel *The Rushes* [1979]), the point to be made by feminist thought on the subject, perhaps almost to the point of obliterating the aforementioned distinction, is the imperative to reject the popular thesis that "women like to be taken by force." Leaving aside the fact that rape is a broader issue than the subjection of women (although women may continue to be the most numerous victims of intimidating violence and the oppression of which violence is a symptom), this popular belief, whereby "no" really means "yes," and "maybe" is an open invitation, is viewed as legitimating the macho fantasy that sexual violence is a privileged norm.

Lynch's novel takes the enormous risk of dealing with a sexual relationship in these terms and of viewing it as a relationship permitted by its victim. That the victim is a woman, the historical majority victim of rape, and that her rapist is a swaggering military despot, makes *Report under Lock and Key* a risky textual undertaking both because it appears, at least on the surface, to sustain the irreflective legitimacy of sexual violence, and to portray sexual violence facilely in terms of a conquering macho and an acquiescing hysterical neurotic who actually seems to welcome his bearlike embraces and views only as unfortunate his intimation that more intense onslaughts are in store for her. The following passage is the end of the text left by Adela, and the trajectory from being a victim of sexual violence to becoming a disappeared person as a victim of destructive military despotism is readily apparent whereby both instances of victimization are homologized as a sustained rape scene:

> Vargas and I coupled until we attained maximum pleasure, and the setting is a tangle of torn blouses, skirts hiked up to the neck, a pants zipper shamelessly undone, and a violence undertaken in God knows in what regions.

> (Vargas y yo nos acoplamos hasta el máximo placer y el cuadro es un revuelo de blusas rasgadas, de polleras enrolladas a la altura del cuello, de un pantalón abierto sin pudor y de una violencia ejercida vaya a saber en nombre de qué regiones.) (298)

Whether Adela is possessed or not by hallucinations at the end of her report (if she is, in fact, carted off under orders of the executive, how is she to have written these words and how can she have gotten them to Ackerman?) does not significantly alter the nature of the events that Adela reports as having *experienced*. But what are we to make of the declaration, "I don't want you to leave me" (No quiero que se vaya de mí)? This would, in fact, seem to be the key to the novel and the lead given to us to work through its structure of far-fetched narrative situations.

Let us begin the consideration of its implications by defining the novel in broad "allegorical" terms; I don't quite like this use of allegory, but it is useful for underscoring how the text reaches at every turn for a larger meaning than the substance of the relationship as such between Adela and Vargas. Perhaps figurative would be a more proper adjective here, to the extent that a relationship on one level (the human, involving a sexual coupling) is also a meaningful relationship on another level (the political, involving a sociohistoric dynamic). But then, ideological readings of narratives usually involve discovering such patterns of reduplication, so the precise term to describe them is not all that important.[10]

On the political level, the relationship between Adela and the executive involves the fictional inscription of the sociohistorical relationship between Argentina and its military establishment. This proposition could lead to all sorts of reductionist interpretations, the fundamental one being that Argentina is to be viewed as a woman who, in addition to an obsession with the military as a form of macho dominance, does in fact enjoy being periodically raped. That such rape is wont to involve mortal orgasm—the little death made final—is only part of the sexual excitement of that relationship. In this nuclear interpretation, there is no way to explain the Argentine tolerance for the rape (which hereby becomes an expanding metaphor for all of the varieties of violence—physical, psychological, sociopolitical) at the hands of the military. That the military is sanctified by the hierarchy of Argentina's semiofficial religion—the famous blessing of the swords by the church primate during the military dictatorship—is one ritualistic metonymy of the institutionalization of the military as a legitimate source of power in the country, one that has historically come to be the dominant one. The way in which the military has achieved this legitimated

10. Jameson, "Pleasure: A Political Issue," 12–14; Peter Bürger, *Teoría de la vanguardia*, 130–36.

primacy may be the only way to explain how the country had, by the 1970s, come to tolerate successive waves of military tyranny, despite the manifest ineptitude of the dictatorships ever to resolve any of Argentina's abiding problems: returns to democracy had become only strategic retrenchments whenever that ineptitude becomes acutely apparent, as for example so dramatically after the Malvinas debacle.

If the foregoing appears to wander alarmingly from the text of *Report under Lock and Key*, it is only because the relationship between Adela and Vargas, so outrageous on the surface, can only begin to make sense if the literal text can be freed to explore the ways in which its meaning beyond the far-fetched correlates with the processes of history in which, throughout the novel, Vargas is in fact involved as a collaborator. Adela, of course, may be seen as merely one more in a legion of heroines in Argentine fiction whose neurotic hysteria (*pace* feminist exceptions about such a stereotype) may point to a horrible abyss of human/social experience or may, after all, be nothing but rambling delusions of persecution. Indeed, *Report under Lock and Key* seems to have borrowed a page from Ernesto Sabato's *Sobre héroes y tumbas* (*On Heroes and Tombs*, 1963), in which the healthfully normal protagonist Martín can only get on with his life when he has put the terrible story of Alejandra's incestuous involvement with her father and the secret sect of the blind behind him, and, presumably, out of his mind. Yet it is not all that clear that Alejandra is simply raving, and like those horror films where the audience may be brought up short after having begun to believe that the creatures from beyond the grave or out of the deep don't really exist after all and that it may then really be true (say, the fundamental ambiguity with which *Rosemary's Baby* leaves us), Martín's "return to normalcy" may in reality be more an act of delusion than Alejandra's weird tale. Martha Mercader in *Solamente ella* (Only her, 1981) tells the story of a woman singer who falls victim to military repression within the context of the continuities between political repression and the oppression of women in macho-dominated societies, and Enrique Medina in *With the Gag in Her Mouth* also strives for the same sort of correlation on the basis of an Argentine hierarchy of patriarchal authoritarianism, of which the military is only one dramatic manifestation. Mercader's woman, like Adela, becomes a victim of disappearance, while Medina's female protagonist rebels by castrating her swaggering boyfriend with the blade of a straight razor.

It is important to attend to the concluding pages of Lynch's novel, in which the framing narrator returns to tell of Ackerman's attempt to trace Adela's whereabouts:

> Ackerman visited Vargas and was surprised to find him an amiable person, concerned as one might expect with Adela's whereabouts. He was surrounded by a normal setting, with no sign of luxury or stridency, very different from anything perceived by the anxious observation of the girl. Nor did he seem to be perverse. The only thing that broke the general harmony was his nervous habit of chewing on the edge of his left hand. His office was nothing more than a workplace, and in no way did he appear to be anything but a busy man. He was sympathetic with Ackerman and alluded vaguely to dangers and casualties, such that the psychiatrist took his leave convinced that this was a dead end.

> (Ackerman visitó a Vargas y se sorprendió al encontrar a una persona amable, normalmente preocupada por el destino de Adela. Estaba rodeado de un ambiente normal, sin lujos ni estridencias, muy distinto de todo cuanto había aparecido ante la observación ansiosa de la muchacha. Tampoco parecía perverso; sólo rompía la armonía general su nerviosa costumbre de mordisquear el canto de su mano izquierda. La oficina no era sino un lugar de trabajo y él mismo en nada era distinto de un hombre muy atareado. Demostró simpatía por Ackerman y aludió vagamente a peligros y casualidades, de tal modo que el siquiatra se marchó con el convecimiento de que esa vía estaba cerrada.) (301; original italicized)

This is the penultimate paragraph; in the last paragraph the narrator informs us that Vargas perishes with his retinue in a plane crash, from which one may conclude that he too becomes a disappeared person in the military's ongoing internal power struggle.

While this final paragraph could be read as vitiating Adela's confessions of perverse erotic attachment to Vargas and her conclusion that she is being persecuted, it would also vitiate any attempt to balance the far-fetchedness that I have attributed to the novel's plot circumstances by correlating it with an overt political meaning. Such a vitiation would turn *Report under Lock and Key* into the ravings of a hysterically and erotically obsessed woman completely divorced from the reality of her situation, which would presumably be a casual affair with a high-ranking but otherwise pedestrian military official. But of course, Lynch's narrator (who signs herself as Marta Lynch) is necessarily speaking here with the same irony as at the end of her initial fragment, where she speaks about how Argentines have learned how to view their "thirst for justice" (sed de justicia). The key to this irony is when she picks up on the indirectly quoted psychiatrist's use of the term "muchacha" to describe Adela and when she slyly characterizes the immediate man-to-man relationship that arises between the two professional men, psychiatrist and military officer, the latter "normally preoccupied" over the fate of his former lover. With a male discourse of polite and reassuring professionalism quickly having been established between Ackerman and Vargas that leaves no room for any plausibility for Adela's discourse, the psychiatrist withdraws with the self-assurance that this cannot have been the sign spoken by his patient's text. It is immaterial whether Adela's text is hysterical or not: such a characterization is nothing but a tactic to divert attention from what is important, which is whether or not it is true as regards the facts of her experience and their implications. Like the characterization as hysterical of human rights denouncements of persecution, torture, and death under military dictatorships, to call Adela's text hysterical is to make a stylistic judgment rather than to assign it a truth value. And since it is a female discourse that is involved, it is disconsonant with the exclusionary male, professional discourse of Ackerman, Vargas, and others, which confines it to the nonmeaningful, the nonsensical. And lest the point get lost, Adela is as much a victim of Ackerman as she is of Vargas: both subject her to tortuous psychological experiences, with Vargas's aggressions apparently finally becoming physical in nature. Adela's sense of being obliged to write for Vargas is matched by her need to write for Ackerman, and both derive a measure of their professional self-identification from the writing that she produces at their imperious behest; and, of course, both survive her and her writing with their professional identities apparently intact.

Moreover, by beginning with a narrative plot that is on its surface far-fetched, Lynch openly challenges the metric of conventional verisimilitude, just as do those accounts where individuals (those who represent the "feminine" that both falls outside of and is, mostly as a consequence of being on the outside, persecuted/raped/obliterated by the dominant "masculine") are shown to be victims of self-legitimating tyranny. The risks that Lynch takes with her novel are, however, not so much of being dismissed as far-fetched. The audaciousness of the attempt to chart the relationship between the feminine and the masculine, between Argentina and the military, and between what is characterized by the masculine as feminine neurotic hysteria in the process of justifying the rape of "women" by "men" (the quote marks refer here to the resulting cultural constructs rather than to biology), makes *Report under Lock and Key* as susceptible to being dismissed as hysterical as Adela's confessions are or as human rights reports are. The use of an erotic relationship, one that the female protagonist characterizes as being built on the fatal attraction of rape, first the threat of it and then its real enactment and culminating in her disappearance, gives *Report under Lock and Key* a morbid fascination, and a secondary risk is in its being read with the same embarrassed relish that the so-called normal bring to pornography and its forbidden fruits. Yet it is precisely in the challenge to read Lynch's novel as a fictional inscription of a historical dynamic—Argentina's obsession with military tyranny and the violations that subsequently accompany it—that makes it one of the most interesting political novels of the last round of Argentine dictatorships.

Yet there is another aspect of *Report under Lock and Key* that must be dealt with, if only summarily, and that is the inevitable slippage in meaning that accrues to the neoallegorical or perhaps more properly figurative mode in which Lynch casts her fiction. Should readers accept the fact that the novel is a transcoding as a violent erotic relationship of apparent Argentine acquiescence to, if not passion for, military authoritarianism, it would seem reasonable that they would in turn want to know why it is proposed that such a pattern best be understood as an erotic perversion, or, if not as a perversion, at least as an obsession. To be sure, from one point of view, such a scheme can be read in strictly allegorical terms, whereby one meaning is only "conveniently" represented by some other one, for reasons of stylistic elaboration or, perhaps, in this case for reasons of censorship: "to say in another way" is the consequence of not being able to call things by their own name. In a more properly figurative mode, however, the two structures of signification are alleged to enjoy a nonarbitrary link between them, whereby the process of semiosis moves back and forth between one and the other as intrinsically conjoined in mutual signification. The binary opposition of Eros versus civilization does not help much in the case of Lynch's novel, since erotic love and civilized authoritarianism are, rather than being disjunctive categories, in fact joined: authoritarianism has become a form of eroticism. And it is in this controlling hypothesis that macho violence has become a sort of sexual perversion for Adela/Argentina where *Report under Lock and Key* opens a Pandora's box of psychohistorical interpretation that it ultimately cannot pursue beyond the representation of a set of narrative situations alleged to be symptomatic of it.

CHAPTER 6

Two Feminist Dramatic Versions of Patriarchal Repression

Dolores: Nothing is as simple as you think. Nor is anything as complicated. The straight can be twisted and hunchback as flat as a golden field. *She laughs acidly*

(*Dolores:* Que nada es tan simple como uno cree. Y nada tampoco tan complicado. Que lo derecho puede ser torcido y lo giboso plano como un campo dorado. *Ríe, ácida*)

—Griselda Gambaro
La malasangre

Griselda Gambaro's *La malasangre* and the Dramatic Configuration of an Argentine Historical Principal

One of the constants in contemporary Argentine culture is the contribution to an understanding of national character gained by analyzing the ideological, thematic, or semantic elements surrounding the founding of the republic. Ricardo Piglia's *Respiración artificial* (Artificial Respiration, 1980), Martha Mercader's *Juanamanuela, Quite a Woman*, even Fernando Solanas's film *Los exilios de Gardel* (The exiles of Gardel, 1985), discover preludes in the nineteenth century to the disastrous institutional—and, hence, personal—life experienced by Argentines during the past fifty years. Over and over again, we can find in these signal works, and in the many others that could be named, a postulated continuity between the tyrannies of the past and the dictatorships of the present; the abuses of yesterday and the persecutions of today; the insecurity of life at the dawn of the republic and the cycle of disappearances, tortures, and clandestine kangaroo courts that characterize the so-called dirty war of recent national history.

In the case of the theater, the works presented as part of the first cycle of Teatro Abierto in 1981 are no exception to this way of establishing resonances between the outlines of history and modern contexts, and *El Nuevo Mundo* (The New World) by Carlos Somigliana places the arrival of the Marquis de Sade in South America within the broad spectrum of postulations that, in terms of certain interpretations of European history, underscore its societies. No spectator can have failed to collate Somigliana's dramatic proposal, with its intentional anachronistic touches, with events of the day in Argentina.

Griselda Gambaro's *La malasangre* (Bad blood) opened in August 1982, and there can be no doubt that it belongs to the sort of historical revisionism at issue here. Organized around a series of allusions to the dictatorship of Juan Manuel Rosas (1829–1852) that are impossible to miss—references to the symbolic color red of his Federales followers; the horrifying metaphor of ripe melons for the heads lopped off by the Mazorca, the secret police; the image of the "city on the other side of the river" (Montevideo) as a refuge from repression; even including the populist pronoun *voseo* that Rosas was the first to use in the halls of government—Gambaro's play traces the portrait of a society founded on the arbitrary and bloody exercise of power in the name of a spurious peace and well-being that has profound echoes for the contemporary Argentine and Latin American spectator.

Given the prevailing characterization of Gambaro's plays as Latin American examples of a theater of the absurd, an approach that stresses historical elements could seem to constitute a novel reinterpretation of her theater or better yet, a new direction given by the author herself to her works. Nevertheless, it is well known that Gambaro has frequently repudiated in no uncertain terms the absurdist characterization of her plays by critics. In a certain sense, there is a misunderstanding on both sides, possibly deriving from a difference of rhetorical emphasis. Gambaro insists that her theater cannot be called absurd because she attempts to adhere as faithfully as possible to a strict representation of reality. Like the magical realists who maintain that what might look like fantasy for some incautious readers corresponds, in fact, to the true outlines of daily existence in Latin America, Gambaro (and along with her a broad array of dramatists of the generation that she represents) gives us to understand that what is being acted out in their plays is nothing more nor less than the actual life Latin Americans live. Discourse that is alleged to be absurd is, after all, the true one, and, if we want to understand Latin American society, it is our responsibility to attend to it rather than to the one that would entrap us in official versions. So far so good. But the word "absurd" in contemporary dramatic criticism does not mean fictional and even less escapist, but rather it alludes to a perspective that radically dispenses with the comfortable conventions of naturalist representation in favor of a theatrical discourse that rigorously frames our modern circumstance, no matter how "absurd" it may appear in the light of such conventions.

In any event, by going beyond the spurious disjunction between "absurd" and "realist," one can see the degree to which Gambaro's works focus on questions that echo the social—and historical—issues of Latin America. If *Las paredes* (The Walls, 1966) and *El campo* (The camp, 1968) concern aggression against the individual on the part of the implacable, arbitrary power we associate with military tyrannies, *El desatino* (Foolishness, 1965) and *Los siameses* (The Siamese twins, 1967) plumb the interpersonal dynamic that makes possible our persecution of the Other. *Decir sí* (Saying yes), Gambaro's contribution to Teatro Abierto 1981, underscores the obsequiousness of the individual in the face of repression, an attitude that only serves to reinforce and to aggravate the strategies of repression.

Where *Bad Blood* does in fact differ from Gambaro's previous theater is in the possibility we perceive that overcoming obsequiousness can evolve into the adoption of a position that can enhance the dimensions of human dignity. In this sense, it becomes part of a politics of the individual to say no to arbitrary power. This negative cannot but be tragic, as much in the sense of leading to the punishment and probable annihilation of the individual as in the sense of deriving from an anagnorisis that allows individuals to distance themselves from the degrading circumstance that has led to a state of self-awareness or recognition. Gambaro's works generally attempt to raise the consciousness of the spectator with respect to the destruction of the individual through the abuse of power, leaving as a concluding theatrical image varieties of human beings' screams of despair in the face of the destiny held in store for them and against which all appeals are in vain. By contrast, *Bad Blood* closes with the following declaration by the daughter of the tyrant. Her clandestine lover, Rafael, whose body is deformed but whose spirit is filled with nobility, has ended up as one more cadaver on the garbage heap generated by patriarchal terror:

Father: What have we raised? A viper? Well, we'll see about the poison in your mouth!

Dolores: No you won't! My poison is sweet! A poison I chew on and swallow!

Father: So much the worse for you. Now get to bed, and that's an order!

Dolores *(laughing):* What? Don't you get it, Daddy? You who are so wise. *(Furiously)* No one's giving orders any more! *(With a harsh and guttural voice)* No one's giving any orders to me or about me! There's no longer any beyond to be afraid of! I'm no longer afraid! I'm free!

Father: *(furiously):* Silence! No one is free when I don't want him to be! I'm still giving the orders in this house! I said get to bed!

Dolores: I will never shut my eyes! If you leave me alive, I will never shut my eyes! I will always be awake, watching you, filled with fury, filled with disgust!

(*Padre:*   ¿Qué criamos? ¿Una víbora? ¡Ya te sacaremos el veneno de la boca!

Dolores: ¡No podrás! ¡Tengo un veneno dulce, un veneno que mastico y trago!

Padre: Peor para vos. Ahora a dormir, ¡y es una orden!

Dolores   (*ríe*): ¿Qué? ¿Cómo no te das cuenta, papito? Tan sabio. (*Furiosa*) ¡Ya nadie ordena nada! (*Con una voz áspera y gutural*). ¡En mí y conmigo, nadie ordena nada! ¡Ya no hay ningún más allá para tener miedo! ¡Ya no tengo miedo! ¡Soy libre!

Padre   (*furioso*): ¡Silencio! ¡Nadie es libre cuando yo no quiero! ¡En esta casa, mando yo todavía! ¡Dije a dormir!

Dolores: ¡Jamás cerraré los ojos! Si me dejás viva, ¡jamás cerraré los ojos! ¡Voy a mirarte siempre despierta, con tanta furia, con tanto asco!)[1]

As in most of Gambaro's plays, *Bad Blood* combines references to the arbitrary exercise of power and the degradation of the human being with a feminist conception of the violation of the woman (or of the feminine, including men who have been feminized as the weak Other) by authoritarian power incarnate in the lord and master (i.e., the masculine), whether he be the father, the husband, or any one of his multiple lackeys assigned the role of giving women "the strong hand in a silken glove. That's what ladies require" ([la m]ano fuerte en guante de seda. Es lo que necesitan las damas) (89). But as the father states immediately following this bit of wisdom, as he hears the cart laden down with the latest harvest of *melones* pass by under his window, "And not only the ladies" (Y no sólo las damas), an amplification that gives us to understand that, for the authoritarian-patriarchal tyrant, anyone is an effeminate and queer *damita* (little lady) who by saying yes legitimizes the aggression of power against themselves.

In theatrical terms, *Bad Blood* exemplifies the best of Gambaro's drama. It would be difficult to improve on the precision of the relationship between dramatic action—the role of Dolores as an

---

1. Gambaro, *La malasangre*, 109, hereafter cited parenthetically in the text.

axis of the abusive power of the Father—and language. Gambaro possesses a special talent for the use of a language that constitutes a sort of ruptured naturalism, in the sense of a discourse where the phatic communication of the characters undergoes a process, at times brutally sudden and at times subtly gradual, in which the texture of speech unravels to reveal the profound intentions that lurk beneath the mask of decency and normalcy. What emerges with shocking clarity is all of the malignity of authoritarianism and all of the despair of the individual trapped by the manipulative structures of that authoritarianism.

The consequence of this sort of ruptured naturalism is a dramatic evolution characterized on all levels of scenic language, and not just on the level of the spoken text, by an iterative process of double meaning. The image of a set of circumstances of apparent normality abruptly disappears to reveal the black abyss of arbitrary power. The following scene turns on the first meeting between Dolores and Juan Pedro, the paradigmatic grinning macho, who has been chosen by the Father to be his daughter's husband:

> Juan Pedro approaches Dolores with his hand outstretched (to invite her to dance the minuet). He looks fleetingly toward her parents and since he sees they are distracted, he brutally touches her breast. Dolores draws away and looks at him stupefied. Juan Pedro, as though the gesture had nothing to do with him, listens for a moment to the music and at a certain point he offers his hand to Dolores. After briefly hesitating, Dolores takes it. They dance.

> (Juan Pedro se acerca a Dolores con la mano tendida [para invitarla a bailar el minué], mira fugazmente hacia los padres y como los ve distraídos, le toca brutalmente un seno. Dolores se aparta y lo mira con estupor. Juan Pedro, como si el gesto no hubiera tenido nada que ver con él, atiende un momento la música y en un punto dado, ofrece su mano a Dolores. Después de una breve vacilación, Dolores la acepta. Bailan). (91–92)

The discourse of double meanings, as much on the level of verbal language as on those of other theatrical registers, makes use of ironic and oxymoronic processes and of sarcastic and contradictory expressions, as well as of strategic inversions of the signifieds. This dramatic modality is pursued always with the purpose of underscoring the distance that exists between the pretensions of peace and well-being of society and the terror that nourishes and sustains them. The guises that these pretensions assume are what Rafael and Dolores, in her tragic understanding at the end of the play, so nobly combat.

It would be inconceivable for a dramatist like Gambaro to be satisfied with staging a play that simply followed the outlines of specific historical events. Although her text has as its backdrop details that are common knowledge with respect to the period of Juan Manuel Rosas (a period that, it is significant to note, the dime novelist Eduardo Gutiérrez recreated under the title of *Los dramas del terror* [The dramas of terror, 1882]), there can be no denying that the meaning of such a play of allusions involves the global sense of authoritarianism and the cynical exercise of power that are constants in Gambaro's theater and narrative. In this sense, it is important to note that *Bad Blood* is a fairy tale in two senses. The unreality of the scenery called for by the text and the playful tone of much of the dialogue, subsequently shattered by the process of calling up the terrifying underlying meanings, could lead one to believe that this play has nothing to do with the published images of the official terrorism of recent events in Argentina. A first impression might be to suppose that *Bad Blood* occupies a cultural space from which the signs of current sociopolitical discourse are absent. But when the spectators are able to begin to grasp the allusions to Rosas's period, they are also able to begin to understand how Rosas put in place in Argentine national life a series of historical constants, with the result that the spectators are then in a position to attend to the echoes of an abiding authoritarian–patriarchal language in the speeches of the Father and to see evidence of the behavior of parapolice organizations and hired assassins in Fermín, the lackey and right-hand man of the Father. In this way, the subtext of *Bad Blood* begins to emerge as a scrupulous portrait of a contemporary reality.

The other sense in which *Bad Blood* is reminiscent of a fairy tale is in the conjunction of apparent normality with a transcendental meaning that reveals to us the hidden motives of human beings. The story of the capricious princess, the long-suffering Mother/queen, and the tyrannical Father/king does not bring to mind the atemporal world of ogres and dashing saviors (in effect, Rafael is *not* able to save Dolores from her tragic destiny), but rather a radically historical context, to the extent that it evokes structures of power that continue to prevail in the society of the spectator.

In the world, in our absurd world as represented by Gambaro's realism, the degradation of the Other by means of authoritarian power is transitive: it becomes transferred from the victimizer to the victim, who in turn becomes a new victimizer with his own victim, and so on endlessly. It is for this reason that the Mother, humiliated over and over again by the Father, can assimilate and assume the latter's power to such an extent that she ends up denouncing the clandestine lovers and their plan to flee to the city on the other side of the river:

> Dolores *(containing her exasperation, as though attempting to explain a commonplace):* That's what happens, Mommy. When you decide for others, that's what happens, things get out of control and no one gets punished. Then you pretend that nothing happened and everyone goes to sleep in the dark, and since the sun doesn't fall out of the sky, you say the next day: nothing happened.

> (*Dolores* [con exasperación contenida, como si intentara una explicación común]: Es lo que pasa, mamá. Cuando se decide por los otros, es lo que pasa, se escapa todo de las manos y el castigo no pertenece a nadie. Entonces, uno finge que no pasó nada y todo el mundo duerme en buena oscuridad, y como el sol no se cae, al día siguiente uno dice: no pasó nada.) (108)

"Nothing's happening here" (Acá no pasa nada . . .): the victims are willing to say yes to the authoritarian Father in order to continue to believe that nothing is wrong—or, that anything that is wrong is happening to the Other, the savage, the degenerate, the antisocial misfit—and they are ready also to make themselves into victimizers in order to go on believing that nothing is wrong. As an example of solidly and unimpeachably historical theater, *Bad Blood* avails itself of all of the resources of Gambaro's brilliant dramatic talent to establish unmistakably the possibility, at a time born of despair become revelation, of saying no: "*Dolores [her voice breaking and unrecognizable]:* The silence is screaming! I say nothing, but the silence is screaming!" (*Dolores [con una voz rota e irreconocible]:* ¡El silencio grita! ¡Yo me callo, pero el silencio grita!) (110). The controlling oxymoron leads us to understand that discourse is still fractured speech, that it continues to be little more than political slogans. But as a form of speaking, of saying, that categorically refutes the obsequiousness of the victim, it is a reasonable place to begin a revision of the sociopolitical process.

Polymorphic Identities: Sexual Theater in Susana Torres Molina's *Extraño juguete*

PERLA: But what kind of salesman are you!
MAGGI: Ladies, I haven't come here to play. . . .
(PERLA: ¡Pero qué clase de vendedor es usted!
MAGGI: [. . .] Señoritas, yo no estoy aquí para jugar . . .)
—Susana Torres Molina, *Extraño juguete*

Extraño juguete (Strange toy) enjoyed more than one hundred performances in 1977.[2] The male lead of Maggi, an amalgam of salesman, magician, and illusionist, was played by Eduardo Pavlovsky, who was at that time Torres Molina's husband and already a firmly established figure in the Argentine theater because of his work as an actor, dramatist, and analyst known for his commitment to the therapeutic uses of psychodrama. Perla was played by Beatriz

2. Zayas de Lima, *Diccionario de autores teatrales argentinos,* 274–75, provides information on the success of Torres Molina's work.

Matar, in whose Taller Actoral Torres Molina had studied; the third role, that of Angélica, belonged to Flora Steimberg. The work opened on July 20, 1977, at the Teatro Payró, a theater that had served as the base for many important Argentine works during the 1970s and is now one of the satellite houses of the Teatro Municipal General San Martín; Oscar Cruz directed *Strange Toy*.

These details from the play's program served to make *Strange Toy* one of the most important works of the Proceso at a time when the Argentine theater was experiencing a notable decline as a consequence of censorship.[3] During this period of the Proceso, marked by disappearances, routine torture, and the liquidation of alleged subversives—all against the backdrop of bloody internecine feuding within the military establishment itself as various branches and factions vied for power—precious few works were able to overcome the suffocating conditions imposed by the ideology of the Proceso and its practical effects on artistic expression and open dialogue in general. Probably the only other significant exception to the depressing situation in the theater is Ricardo Monti's *La visita* (The visit, 1978);[4] Monti wrote one of the two prefatory notes to Torres Molina's text, the other one belonging to Pavlovsky himself.

Set in the present, *Strange Toy* is built around three characters: two women and a man. Because the play functions as a play-within-a-play, the identity of the three characters is distributed on three levels: (1) who they are in relation to the text they are in the process of performing (a complex of roles that is not revealed to the spectator until the final minutes of the play); (2) who they are as individuals who take on the performance of the aforementioned circumstantial text, at the same time they are actors in the play called *Strange Toy*; and (3) who they are as theatrical signs with a semantic weight that results from their participation in the "strange toy" of theatricalized life.

We can easily dispense with the obvious comments on life as drama and the world as theater, along with observations on human

3. Charles B. Driskell, "Theatre in Buenos Aires: 1976–1977."
4. Foster, "Semantic Relativity in Ricardo Monti's *La visita.*"

relations as a dynamic of theatrical interaction and the personality of the human being as a series of ludic masks worn before society as a scrutinizing audience.[5] Contemporary theater affords us with a wide array of these and other similar metatheatrical formulas that confirm how the theater only serves to formalize in an overdetermined way the inescapable nature of human relations. Thus, the primordial function of the spectator is to bring into view in the privileged space of the theater, in a coherent fashion, the disperse elements of a dramatic human interaction. The structures of power, which may be only dimly recognized in the fray of daily life, are expounded with startling clarity in the theater. (This juxtaposition overrides for the purposes of this argument all of the not inconsequential difficulties of transcending the obfuscations of daily life and being able to grasp the clarity the theater offers as a contestatorial reading of the social text.) The metatheatrical element to be found in so many contemporary works is designed to underscore this sociocultural role of the spectacle. It would be superfluous to say that such a relationship assumes greater emphasis in a society experiencing a protracted period of national life when official ideologies have sought to conceal the basic sense of the forces of power, thereby forcing cultural artifacts to assume a demystifying and oppositional posture.

The foregoing general scheme of the theater–life binomial is encoded in the text of *Strange Toy* in terms of the reversible identities attributed to the persons–characters–actors distributed among the various levels that have been described. When one undertakes a rereading of the play from the perspective of the final curtain, it becomes evident that the play is constructed around the compact metaphor of the theater as an example of commercialized, consumer culture. Two women of "high society" (de alta sociedad) pay a starving actor,[6] who humbly begs for a small adjustment in the fee to which he had initially agreed, to organize for them a theatrical spectacle in which they assume the role of two loony

5. Jacqueline Eyring Bixler, "Games and Reality on the Latin American Stage."
6. Torres Molina, *Extraño juguete*, 75, hereafter cited parenthetically in the text.

spinster sisters who fall victim to the salacious abuse of a traveling salesman. The two women appear willing to pay the actor whatever he demands in order for the spectacle to be realistic, so much so that at the end of the work they go over the bills for the scenery, the props, the costumes, and the hours the actor has spent in preparing the text and practicing it. Moreover, just as he is about to take his leave, he offers his two clients a new routine—although he says, with all of the unctuous modesty of the salesman facing demanding clients, that he's not altogether certain it will be to their liking. This is because the two have shown themselves to be dissatisfied with the ending of the "production" he has just conducted for them: precisely at the moment when he is supposed to "spank their little bottoms" for misbehaving, the actor suddenly abandons the stage compelled by physiological necessities, which only serves to destroy the dramatic tension that has built up to that moment:

> MAGGI: (*Overwhelmed.*) My bladder was bursting. I couldn't wait!
>
> ANGELICA: Come on, Mr. Miralles, you're not a little boy!
>
> MAGGI: (*Making amends.*) If you want. . . . Let's start all over.
>
> PERLA: Don't play dumb, OK?
>
> ANGELICA: You've ruined our evening.
>
> (MAGGI: [*Apabullado.*] Me explotaba la vejiga. ¡No daba más!
>
> ANGELICA: ¡Vamos, señor Miralles, no es un chico!
>
> MAGGI: [*Conciliador.*] Si ustedes quieren . . . Volvemos atrás.
>
> PERLA: No se haga el tonto, ¿eh?
>
> ANGELICA: Nos arruinó la noche.) (71)

The night that Maggi/Sr. Miralles has ruined for them is the complicated and sophisticated spectacle that he has created for their enjoyment. In the fashion of the Renaissance masques that dramatists wrote on consignment from the court so that ladies and gentlemen of the nobility could make the transition from watching as spectators to performing as actors, Maggi/Miralles's spectacle is nothing more nor less than a very expensive divertissement for two upper-class women who have grown weary of the canasta and tea parties and who have decided to seek new alternatives for their enjoyment. At the end of the play, both the purveyor of dramatic tableaux and his clients strike an agreement for his future services and the women avail themselves of their position as buyers to impose a clear understanding of the conditions of a healthy professional relationship:

ANGELICA:	(*Authoritatively.*) Mr. Miralles!
MAGGI:	Yes, ma'am.
ANGELICA:	I'm warning you: be on time.
MAGGI:	(*Obsequiously.*) Yes, ma'am.
PERLA:	And please do me the favor of showing up in a clean shirt.
MAGGI:	Yes, ma'am. Of course. Good afternoon.

(ANGELICA:	[*Autoritaria.*] ¡Señor Miralles!
MAGGI:	Sí, señora.
ANGELICA:	Le advierto, sea puntual.
MAGGI:	[*Obsecuentemente.*] Sí, señora.
PERLA:	Y hágame el favor de venirse con una camisa limpia.
MAGGI:	Sí, señora. Por supuesto. Buenas tardes.) (76)

This ending of *Strange Toy* evokes for the spectator all of the images associated with the humble servility of a vast socioeconomic stratum that must rely for its survival on the friendly disposition of individuals like Perla and Angélica, two women who appear to have been brought up to believe that they are as precious and divine as their respective names. One can manage to survive, if not always have a clean shirt, by appealing successfully to the material needs and psychological demands of the Perlas and the Angélicas. There is no need to abound in details as to how such a relationship reduplicates, beyond the generalized economic structure of capitalist societies, the situation of art, in which the rigorous scrutiny of the most hidden recesses of human dynamics is only possible if high-society women are prepared to entertain themselves with such scrutiny and to pay the cost required to make it possible. While this version of basic theatrical structures may be rather parodic, it is nonetheless sufficiently verisimilar to reveal how it brings together concepts of capitalist culture as something feminine, superfluous, merely entertaining, and cut to the fashion of the moment. That Argentina was at the time going through yet another renewed phase of law-of-the-jungle neoliberalism, the so-called *plata dulce* (sweet money) regime imposed by José A. Martínez de Hoz, the Proceso's aristocratic Minister of Economy, provides yet additional resonance to this play. Concomitantly, the enormous growth in Argentina's advertising industry in the mid-1970s, in part to match the development of color television and its definitive penetration into virtually every Argentine home, is an added dimension of Maggi's profession as a salesman of sublime erotic scriptings within a disingenuous system of cultural meanings.

However, *Strange Toy* is more than a skillful and ingenious version of the theater as a cultural phenomenon financed by the upper bourgeoisie to shake up its feelings without bringing about any sort of fundamental change in the structures that support it. If it were only a case of this sort of commentary, the work would merely serve to underscore the bases of its own condition at a time in Argentine social history when the dictatorship was attempting to reaffirm a purified capitalism in the form of a classic market economy favoring a well-demarcated entrepreneurial class.

Beyond pointing the audience to a socioeconomic context that includes the circumstances of the original production of *Strange Toy*, the work is centered on the reversibility of identity of the characters/actors within a power dynamics. If the frame of reference that ultimately prevails in *Strange Toy* alludes to the primary conditions of capitalist culture, the most fascinating aspect of the text resides in the type of spectacle that the two women are willing to pay for. The presupposition that the scripts they have requested will be mirrors of the society in which they live (just as the Renaissance masques tended to be either replicas of the court setting or transpositions of the latter to alternate idealized settings, as in the case of pastoral variants) turns out to be contravened when one realizes that Perla and Angélica agree to be transported to a fantasy world that is the complete counterimage of their social standing.

The two sisters in Miralles's play are old maids who inhabit the run-down paternal home in a supposedly remote Buenos Aires suburb. They live a boring life where only the weak-minded Angélica's outrageous extravagances disrupt the implacable everyday routine. Perla claims to have once held a position as accountant in a business. But when their parents died (one soon after the other, because they were very close), she gave up her job to devote herself to keeping house and caring for the unfortunate Angélica.

One of Angélica's many foolishnesses is to be overly trustful. Thus, one day when a traveling salesman comes to the door, it is Angélica who receives him enthusiastically because she is interested in all of the gadgets he has to offer. Perla finds herself frustrated in her attempt to chase him from the house and, fed up, she accepts Angélica's idea to alleviate the boredom of their lives a little bit by picking through Maggi's merchandise and listening to his persuasive line of patter. The relationship between the three evolves in the course of Maggi's visit. If initially the man is circumscribed by the formulas of speech and behavior of the humble traveling salesman, a transformation in his personality begins to take place at one point until he has been changed into the figure of an abusive intruder who attempts to take advantage of two bored spinsters who have allowed him into their modest home. Alternating the violence of the homicidal rapist with the winning charm of a threadbare shop owner, Maggi weaves a seductive, fascinating text around Perla and Angélica with himself as the central character. He throws out detail after detail concerning his experiences as a traveling salesman, his impoverished and ill-fortuned youth, and the aggressions permitted him thanks to his access to poor lonely women like the two of them: "You understand who I'm referring to?" (¿Ustedes entienden a quienes me refiero?) (63); "You know what I'm talking about, right?" (Ustedes saben de lo que estoy hablando, ¿no es cierto?) (63). Immediately after these interrogatives, he obliges them to participate in the erotic psychodrama he has prepared for them (71).

This scene of gross erotic fantasy terminates ridiculously when Maggi can no longer resist the need to go to the bathroom, a necessity that has made his movements clumsy as he wields the switch with which he attempts to direct the movements of the "actresses," and it is the culmination as much of the way in which the perverse traveling salesman treats the two hysterical spinsters as it is of the dramatic text that Miralles has prepared for them with such great care—even though the two women, in a vulgar imitation of the demands that upstanding, fine women always accord themselves as a natural right, complain about the minor modifications that Miralles has made in the text without informing them (73). The trajectory followed by the three actors synthesizes an abusive relationship, one of exploitation and submission in which the man takes advantage of the solitude of two women forgotten and marginalized by society. The way in which he treats them is humiliating and degrading, even if it is only possible as a consequence of the self-image of the two abandoned women, who goad him on. As a psychodramatic nucleus, the relationship between Maggi and the two sisters emphasizes a rape that is as much physical as it is psychological, one that is permitted within the parameters of the condition of the three as marginal beings in a so-called decent society that Perla and Angélica strive to exemplify in the order and respectability of their home and to which the salesman aspires to be of service in the guide of the products he hawks. The transition from the props of bourgeois decency to a verbal and kinesic discourse that plays on the issues of dependency and exploitation between man and woman, between aggressor and victim, personified in the figure of Maggi as the rapist of women who hide behind doors, underscores a profound interpersonal dynamic that lies beneath the surface of the nice manners displayed by the salesman and his clients.

Nevertheless, the clear outlines of this psychodrama, the perfect image of the abusive exploitation to which the many helpless victims of our society are daily subjected, end up fragmented when the spectators discover that everything they have been witness to is simply a minor divertissement paid for by two high-society ladies whose character, detail by detail, is quite the opposite from that of the two madwomen Perla and Angélica who, were they really to exist, would only with great difficulty find employment in the homes of the women who contract Miralles's services.

It is in a rupture in this transition between the two natures of Perla and Angélica where *Strange Toy* assumes its greatest interest as a theatrical work. In the first place, this fracture invites one to engage in a meditation on the conditions under which theatrical representation takes place. And in the second place, the greatest interest of *Strange Toy* from the point of view of dramatic texture lies precisely in the foreshadowings of this break.

The discourse between Maggi the salesman and his two clients is a series of foreshadowings of the fragmentation of the text and the transition to the metatheatrical level of *Strange Toy*. Moreover, the vaguely nonverisimilar nature of the text that is performed in accord with the comments by Pavlovsky (7–8) serves to prefigure the rupture that will occur at the moment in which Maggi/Miralles can't stand it any longer and rushes off to the bathroom. These foreshadowings provide the speeches of the three actors with the strange texture that characterizes the play, defamiliarizing the interpersonal discourse as a verbal trace of the struggle for power articulated by the relationship between them. As a consequence, what is on the surface the circumstantial contact between a traveling salesman and some rather deranged women clients turns into a conversation in which banal language reveals the possibility of a constellation of signifieds that are markedly disconcerting and dangerous. One can descry a pattern of relations between Maggi and the women that breaks with the circumstantial relationship between them to become transformed into the unchartered territory of terror and the taboo. The backing away at the moment of treading this psychic abyss, far from being a hesitation in the face of the last step necessary to enter fully into the truly strange game, is what allows for the fracture of the drama that has been set in motion and the contemplation on the part of the spectator of the implications, not of the abyss in the relationship of power, but of the mirror effect, of the *mettre en abîme,* that enables the theatrical game in all of its multiple levels of existence within the outlines of our social life.

This texture, which takes on importance as an accumulation of foreshadowings of the fracture that must take place in order to give way to the Brechtian contemplation on the part of the spectator of the theatrical event, extends from the low-level verbal formulas of the characters to whole blocks of speeches that intersect with each other. For example, again and again Maggi closes a hackneyed observation or an insinuating affirmation with the epiphonema "What can I tell you?" (Qué quiere que le diga . . .) and its variants. This phrase punctuates his discourse, first as a crutch and then as a sustained echo of how the salesman, after all, strives to say what the client wants him to say, and finally as a sign of the simple fact that his speech can be no more than a matter of saying what he is told to say.

Within the bilevel expressive framework of *Strange Toy,* every dialogue in which the characters engage takes on a secondary meaning. Even when the spectator is unaware of the true nature of the game, she or he senses that what is being witnessed is much more than the conversation of two bored spinsters and a traveling salesman whose commercial line is transformed into a macabre threat. Within this double framework even the most trivial commonplaces are attended to in terms of their suggestive power, since the scheme that we perceive necessarily lies beyond the surface we experience directly: "Always the same old story. You never change" (Siempre con las mismas pavadas. No cambiás nunca) (16), "Haven't you been here before?" (¿Usted no estuvo antes por aquí?) (21), "Sir, I don't think we understand each other" (Señor, parece que no nos entendemos) (22), "What do you mean?" (¿Qué quieres decir?) (26), "But what kind of salesman are you!" (¡Pero qué clase de vendedor es usted!) (26), "I have no reason to lie to you" (Para qué les voy a mentir) (33), just to mention some random examples from the opening pages of the text. These phrases enjoy a double expressiveness: on the one hand, they are part of a phatic speech with which the characters flesh out their dialogue in imitation of colloquial, daily speech; on the other hand, they are brief indexes of how there is another operant level of meaning where it is important to attempt to determine what kind of salesman Miralles is, what same stupidities as always are involved, and exactly *what* it is that he means.

Additionally, there are various blocks of dialogue where desynchronized exchanges, in addition to being radically disconcerting for the spectator, cannot help but alert one to the scheme that will only be revealed toward the end of the spectacle. For example, at one moment the salesman becomes frustrated over the apparent lack of interest on the part of the two women and leaves:

MAGGI: May I tell you something? I'm fed up! Good afternoon. *(He closes the door and leaves.)*

ANGELICA: *(To Perla.)* Congratulations! You get better every day.

PERLA: Thanks, dear. Your company is what inspires me.

(MAGGI: [. . .] ¿Quiere que les diga una cosa? ¡Estoy harto! Buenas tardes. *[Cierra la puerta y se va.]*

ANGELICA: *[A Perla.]* ¡Te felicito! Cada día lo hacés mejor.

PERLA: Gracias, querida. Tu compañía me inspira.)   (27)

Both Maggi's outburst of anger and the two women's self-congratulatory gestures fall outside the "tone" of the exchange of speeches that have been developed up to this point, and this brief alteration in the discursive parameters will subsequently take on, in a context of retrospective reflection, an indexical value of the true "theatrical" relationship between the characters. The same function could be attributed to the exchange of opinions concerning the nighttime job that Maggi claims to have, where "the clientele is different. It's a different public" (la clientela [. . .] es otra. [. . .] Es otro público) (45). Another example occurs when there is a prelude to the erotic game that closes the commissioned spectacle, when the comings and goings of the two sisters are cut short by the unexpected declaration of the salesman:

MAGGI: So, you want to yank me around! Who do you think
you're dealing with? Twenty-five years working the
streets like a jerk! So, you like the party? OK, then we'll
have us some fun.

(MAGGI: Así que tiene ganas de joder, ¡eh! ¿Pero quién se creen
que soy? ¡Veinticinco años laburando en la calle de bo-
balicón! ¿Así que les gusta la fiesta? Y bueno, vamos a
divertirnos.)   (68)

Other elements that exercise a similar foreshadowing role, in
so much as they insinuate a double level of meaning, the phatic
versus the scandalous, are the rhetorical questions, the enigmas
that remain unanswered, and the absurd sequences within the
norm of grotesque local color that makes up the basic nature of
the encounter between the salesman and the two spinsters. We
have already described how Maggi's absurd need at one point to
satisfy pressing physiological needs triggers the transition from one
level to another within the dramatic text. The absurd note of the
interplay between the characters in the face of Maggi's anecdotes,
one more clumsily macabre than the last, provides an element of
perplexity for the attentive spectator who may feel frustrated in
the face of the difficulty, if not the impossibility, to piece together
everything that is being presented on stage. Thus, when Perla
demands: "And, just who's Mr. Maggi? (*Angelica does not answer.*)
Come on, tell me, what is he?" (¿Y el señor Maggi, quién es?
[*Angélica no contesta.*] ¿A ver, decime, qué es?) (43), the spectator
must necessarily focus on the interrogative *what* and not on the
expected *who*, to begin the process of discovering that Maggi is
much more than he appears to be.

In sum, these elements of prefiguration undermine the merely
wacky facade of the encounter between the salesman and his clients
and look toward the installation of the scheme of relations that are
not developed with any sort of specificity until toward the end of
the play. In retrospect, the spectator recontextualizes, resemantizes
these declarations within the interplay of the text dictated by the
two high-society denizens.

Yet when all is said and done, we have insisted that the true meaning of *Strange Toy* is not to be found in the text that the dramatist-for-hire sets up, nor in the "return to reality" that takes place when the women pay Miralles off for his theatrical services. Rather, it is to be found in the point of cleavage between the two when the spectator is asked to meditate, less on the power Perla and Angélica possess to command dramatic performances and more on why the spectacle for which they pay is like it is. In the "real" world they belong to the group that marks the transition from society, disposing and ordering at will in a sustained exercise of socioeconomics that is as arbitrary as it is unimpeachable, but in the world of the two spinsters they find themselves exposed to the aggressions of a depraved rapist who plays without pity on their weaknesses as individuals forgotten and marginated by society. As the contemplation of the abyss of the exploiters, as the imperative to undertake a process of erotization whereby one's skin becomes the very locus of the humiliation practiced on the other, the theatrical exercise elaborated by Perla and Angélica is ever more cynical as it becomes the way to overcome the tedium of yet one more boring afternoon. One of the most chilling foreshadowings that punctuate the play serves trenchantly to remind the spectator of the social parameters that obtain beyond the confines of the stage:

> PERLA: They should be turned in. . . .
> MAGGI: With all the work the police stations have on their hands, it's no use!

> (PERLA: Habría que denunciarlos . . .
> MAGGI: Con el laburo que hay ahora en las comisarías, ¡qué va a denunciar!)   (32)

These parameters and the circumstances of daily life of people like Miralles dying from hunger are what make the "strange toy" of Perla and Angélica possible, along with their absolute trust in how such toys can never become reality, that the theater will continue to be nothing more than theater, a provocative game but never a truly threatening proposition. The scenery is struck, the actors are paid off, everybody goes to tea like decent people, and the final curtain falls.

It would be superfluous to insist that *Strange Toy*, as an analysis of this scheme of relations between the theater and social reality, between actors and spectators, in real-life texts and make-believe ones, points toward a process of consciousness-raising both of our society of mass-consumed commercial culture and of the legitimate postulates of a deconstructivist theater. By deconstructing the relation between the salesman of dreams and illusions and his clients, Torres Molina implies a type of theater that will be possible only when we set aside our strange toys. This was achieved in part four years later with the Teatro Abierto movement, but then by this time we are talking about a period of sociocultural revisionism in Argentina that was only dimly to be perceived in the harsh years of the Proceso by daring works like *Strange Toy*.

Torres Molina, who elsewhere was to take on the structures of sexual identity in defiance of the draconian heterosexism of the dictatorship,[7] presents the spectator of *Strange Toy* with a complex theatrical formula in which the relationship between sexual violence and the structures of power, one aspect of which is to command performances of a playfully eroticized but strictly contained theater of social violence, undergoes a process of homologization that demonstrates the degree to which tyrannical sociopolitical power vitiates any threat to its primacy and also becomes a mechanism for ensuring its own triumphal perpetration.

7. Foster, "The Manipulation of the Horizons of Reader Expectation in Two Examples of Argentine Lesbian Writing: Discourse Power and Alternate Sexuality."

CHAPTER 7

Sexual Doing and Being Done
in Gambaro's *Lo impenetrable*

Pornography is so paradigmatically a male-authored genre, meaning also that it is paradigmatically a male-addressed genre, that any such text signed by a woman is immediately host to all sorts of conjectures and problems of interpretation. Furthermore, since in the Western languages pornographic texts are primarily spoken in English or French, the presence of pornography in a so-called Third World language such as Spanish (at least in one of its Latin American dialects, even an "imperial" one like the Argentine literary standard) only compounds the issues suddenly raised by the reckless strangeness of the text.

To be sure, the definition and the explanation of pornography are two sides of one of the thorniest issues of modern culture.[1] Pornography literally means "writing about prostitutes," but its general contemporary usage is any cultural manifestation *taken* by the reader to have fundamentally to do with the practices of sex in a discourse other than the bracketedly scientific; concomitantly, this definition means that something will be judged not to be pornographic if it is perceived that the nonscientific treatment of

1. Maurice Charney, *Sexual Fiction*; Kate Millett, *Sexual Politics*; Angela Carter, *The Sadeian Woman and the Ideology of Pornography*; Walter M. Kendrick, *The Secret Museum: The History of Pornography in Literature*; Susan Griffin, *Pornography and Silence: Culture's Revenge against Nature*; Susan Gubar and Joan Hoff, eds., *For Adult Users Only: The Dilemma of Violent Pornography*; Donald Symons, *The Evolution of Human Sexuality*.

sex is part of a larger human issue, the so-called socially redeeming provision of classic first amendment defenses. Of course, such an approach assumes that there is nothing socially redeeming about pornography as such, which is certainly a signpost of any cultural uneasiness about texts stripped of the moral definitions of sex (for example, Sade and his avatars) and the need to erect a secure ideological disjunction between bad pornography and healthy erotica if one is a "liberal" citizen, and between bad pornography/eroticism and ennobling spirituality if one is "morally conservative." Such binary oppositions make it easy to pigeonhole cultural practices—both the production of texts and their reception/reading as a secondary or projective level of text production—and to draw very neatly the opposing camps in the debate of what should be called pornographic and how to rescue from the cleansing fires what can be shown to be not pornographic but something else that echoes current cultural priorities. The erotica of the material body, as pursued by feminism and lesbian/gay liberation, are among the legitimate priorities of the moment.[2]

The fact that the binary oppositions suggested above can only be ideologically defined and have no absolutely real status has made the task of discrimination essentially a hopeless one. What has emerged in recent decades as a more interesting debate has been the attempt to understand the social and cultural role of anything that can be called pornographic beyond the condemnation of the moralists—although, in all honesty, one must confess that a lot of nontheological denunciations of pornography have tended to take on a moralizing tone, and words like "sinful" and "perverse" have been substituted for by other terms that may have greater sociological specificity but are nonetheless quite synonymous with the language of the legions of decency.

It takes no great intellectual effort to understand why many (but not all) feminists will decry the exploitation of women in pornography; why a gay consciousness will decry the automatized violence of certain acts associated in the public consciousness with

2. Gallop, *Thinking through the Body*; Foster, *Gay and Lesbian Themes*.

homosexuality, whether practiced homosexually or heterosexually in pornographic texts (in addition to lamenting facile equivalencies between the obsession with anonymous sex in pornography and similar attributions to homosexuality); and why ethnic groups must repudiate energetically the narremes of sex slavery, the supercharged foreigner, and the exotic cultural landscapes that are frequent mainstays of pornographic narratives. There is considerable reasonableness in the outrage over these narremes of pornography, especially when they can be read as confirming the fantasies of the oppressive patriarchy regarding sex and its proper agents, and the proper objects of those agents.

Indeed, much of the debate turns on the question of fantasy, of whether pornographic fantasies are the locus of a drama of oppressive power or a form of erotic theatrics in which the issue is not power but various forms of role-playing in a drama of sexual gratification. To be sure, where such dramatic roles can be shown to be strictly homologous with the roles for the exercise of power—sexual, social, political, cultural—in the real world, it is legitimate to say that the text is either faithfully reduplicating a historical situation, and thereby confirming and strengthening it, or it is projecting a general scheme that needs to be more firmly articulated in the real world. Yet it is questionable whether pornographic texts manifest this sort of efficient homology with historical reality. Rather, they seem to be more the stagings of multiple and shifting erotic roles, where the actors can and do effect a dizzying *ars combinatoria* (combinatory art) where the agentive and objective parts, the doer and the done to, only assume a correspondence with the actual power relations of life part of the time and in the context of other combinations that are not customarily those of the real world.

Leaving aside the question of how, outside the predetermined scripts of sexual menus, one clearly determines who is doing and who is being done to, it is worthwhile to consider the possibility that it is only in so-called high-class pornography, pornography with the pretension of serving as a sort of socially redeeming metapornography—the writings of the Marquis de Sade, *The Story of* O, the diaries and stories of Anaïs Nin—where sexual role homologies with historical relations of power are scrupulously pursued, with the intention of producing a pornographic text that will demonstrate how the power relations of a society are reduplicated in actual sexual dynamics. This leaves pornography-as-sexual-fantasies on the margin of what is not explored because it represents combinations other than those that reproduce true-life power politics. This line of reasoning clearly admits a distinction between some pornography as alternate-sexuality fantasies and all pornography as always and necessarily a reduplication of power politics, even when it does confess that a goodly amount of any grab bag of pornographic writings of whatever pretensions will turn on sexual role-taking that neatly matches numerous definitions of the social exploitation of women, children, ethnic groups, and whatever other constituency the critic may be sensitized to.

Much of what Maurice Charney calls "sexual fiction" overlaps with what I have called metapornography. From one point of view, one could insist that these works are what a less generous reader would call high-class pornography or simply the more vicious kind of pornography written for the more refined, and therefore more dangerously debauched, reader than the dirty French postcards in prose designed for mass consumption (one remembers Philip Marlowe's experiences with a private lending library with a "select" well-healed clientele in *The Big Sleep* [1939]). From this point of view, to speak of metapornography is nothing more than a legitimizing tactic, a form of special pleading, for what is after all nothing but pornography, pure and simple.

But where the notion of metapornography acquires a fresh dimension is in a Third World context like Latin America. One can handily dismiss as blue-nose censorship the fulminations against the alleged indecency of really rather circumspect passages in a lot of prose, theater, and motion pictures. In most cases it is so painfully obvious that the author/dramatist/auteur is striving for a homologous representation of power politics that it is safe to assume the critics are really objecting to the graphic portrayal of naked power rather than sex. True, there is the Brazilian *pornochan-chada* (porno + hack play, farce), which is every bit as bad as routine American stag films or queasiness-inspiring combinations of sex and other taboo subjects such as the black arts. Yet the market for pornography in Latin America is for foreign, nowadays predominantly American, products, and one wonders if it is economically feasible for anyone to bother to try to create local products to compete with this slick trade. Indeed, the image of anything American so often approaches the level of sensual aspiration toward the unattainable that it is a form of desired pornographic object, wherein American pornographic products are only one subset of an overall desire-drenched longing. This equation may be straining the limits of credible sociocultural interpretation, but the fact remains that in pornography as in so many other realms of late capitalist consumerism, it is not economically feasible for local productions in Latin America to compete with U.S. and western European productions.

What all this means is that anything that can be identified in Latin America as indigenous pornography, no matter what qualifiers accompany it, is automatically bracketed and subjected to interpretation as "something other than." This may indeed be always the case with what looks like pornography when it is signed by a woman, and it is certainly the case with Griselda Gambaro's *Lo impenetrable* (*The Impenetrable Madam X*, 1984).

Why would a woman write something that a superficial critical glance would identify as pornography? Feminist consciousness could hardly contemplate the possibility that a woman might wish to reduplicate male-centered—male-authored and male-addressed—pornography. (The assignment of a male addressee, it should be noted, is based on strategies of critical reading that are designed to identify the implied and/or ideal reader of a text, no matter who its real readers may be, real readers who may wish for a number of reasons to assume a self-identity with the implied/ideal reader, which is certainly what happens in a lot of cultural production.)

Contrarily, however, this is precisely what seems to be at work in a lot of romance writing, which is primarily authored by women (that is, the Barbara Cartland dynasty). To the extent that the pulp romance is based on images of the "strong" male (*dominant*, *swaggering, lustful,* and other adjectives appear in the publicity, usually accompanied by bronzed and bare-chested illustrations) and the "swooning" female (dependent, frail, besieged, and pale colored), all set against action-filled backdrops that are sexual homologies (that is, love as coterminous with violence), these texts can be called a form of soft pornography, although it is likely that contemporary writing has gotten ever bolder in the depiction of sexual hydraulics and the intentions and emotions associated with them. And a wide array of sensationalistic journalism, a lot of whose content deals with sexual violence, implied or graphic, appears to be bought as often by women as by men. Feminist interpretations customarily attribute the consumption of soft porn and sensationalistic journalism that reproduces images of the violent patriarchal society as demonstrating both the appalling extent of an unconstructed feminist consciousness and, concomitantly, the abiding force of the violent patriarchy, which is, after all, what pornography is judged to be all about.

If it is true that feminism must also deal with the way in which women not only accept their own subjugation by a phallocentric society but also reproduce it in their own cultural production, either out of cynicism (the exploitation of the exploiter) or out of despairing self-defense (pretend to go along with the exploiter to forestall greater exploitation), then it becomes easier to explain why women might sign texts that can be claimed to be the very paradigm of the violent patriarchy. Nevertheless, the strategies of reading that seek to uncover cleverly concealed or perhaps even unintentional undercuttings of the paradigm provide such products with different resonances than male-signed homogeneous texts. Such an undercutting is usually acknowledged to be at work in *The Story of O.* One must add that the same sort of undercutting can certainly occur in male-signed texts, which is what Gallop has perceived to be at work in Sade's writing, often viewed as the zenith of phallocentric culture.

Yet aside from the enormous respect that is likely to accrue to women's writing that superficially looks like it is reproducing the patriarchy but that can be argued to constitute clever underminings of it, it is safer to assume that the compelling reason for a woman to produce what looks like pornography is to burlesque it. Burlesque, as a broadly unsubtle form of satire, allows for the unambiguous and categorical debunking of its pre-text, which, depending on the economy of the text's structure, is laid low with greater or lesser attention to all of the details of its internal structure. Some burlesques are content only to ridicule their pre-text in a general fashion, while others undertake a point-by-point dissection that serves to foreclose any attempt to reinstall the repudiated ideology.

The Impenetrable Madam X is an excellent example of burlesqued pornography. A novel that has gone virtually unnoticed by the field of literary criticism (as has the majority of Gambaro's fiction, unjustly overshadowed by her brilliant theatrical production), *The Impenetrable Madam X* was, according to Gambaro's declaration on the back cover, written in 1980 during her exile in Spain and as a sort of breather from the overwhelming sociopolitical reality of Argentina that was the cause for that exile. Yet it is interesting to meditate on the logical continuities between a sociopolitical reality that has produced, in Gambaro's theater and in her fiction, some of the most wrenching textual rewritings of the violent patriarchy and the use of the structural scheme of pornography, which can be considered the dominant paradigm of violent patriarchy. Indeed, Gambaro's early theater was criticized for being populated essentially by male characters: How was it possible that a feminist playwright would focus almost exclusively on men? In a play like *The Siamese Twins*, the violence is between men,[3] while in *The Camp* it is shown to extend to both women and men in whom the feminine is dominant (that is, men who have not been thoroughly gendered to the sadistic masculine principle of the concentration camp director). In *Foolishness,* a man is the victim of both his macho brother and his mother, in whom the masculine principle prevails in concert with her aggressive son.

3. Foster, "El lenguaje como vehículo espiritual en *Los siameses* de Griselda Gambaro."

These works demonstrate how Gambaro is able to conjugate various combinations of sex and gender roles (obviously having assimilated very well sources parallel to those of the French feminists) and why male roles predominate in her works of the 1960s and early 1970s as the most consistent embodiment of masculine violence, although a woman may embody the masculine principle and a man the feminine one of the integrated body. In Gambaro's theater beginning in the late 1970s, female figures have come to dominate, either in their unfortunately abiding role of manifesting the integrated body shattered by masculine sadism (*Del sol naciente* [The rising sun]) or as assertive agents of a rebellion against patriarchal violence (*Bad Blood* and *Antígona furiosa* [Antigone in Anger]). If Gambaro's contribution to the much vaunted Teatro Abierto 81 cycle was *Saying Yes,* in which a male-to-male aggression reproduces the mutilation of their bodies that the citizenry allows tyrannical regimes to carry out, *Bad Blood* and *Antígona furiosa* are the resounding "Decir *no*" of women (as much the feminine principle as specifically female citizens) who will no longer allow their bodies, including their spirits, to be violated by the patriarchy, which is literally present in both works, the former based on Argentine history, the latter a rewriting of the classical myth (in turn one of Western culture's first examples of feminine rebellion).

The Impenetrable Madam X is most assuredly continuous with Gambaro's previous and subsequent theater (and with fictional works like *Ganarse la muerte* [Earning death] and *Dios no nos quiere contentos* [God does not want us to be happy] also centering on the violent patriarchy). From one point of view, the novel is a lockstep inversion of the formulas of pornography: an aggressive female pursues a demurring male, enveloping him finally in a grip of rape. The object of Madam X's feverish entrapment is suitably elusive and unresponsive, and the partial approaches to him are comic recastings of the literary commonplaces of quest literature. The tone of these accumulated frustrations in attaining her object, despite El Caballero's abundant sexual performances in every context other than with Madam X, is exemplified by the following passage, where Gambaro's burlesque of the purple prose of "serious" pornography writing is quite evident:

"W.5!" she shouted, perceiving an answer in the form of a sound she knew all too well. The gentleman shuddered, doubled over, crouching more and more until Madam X could no longer see his head. She stood up, trying to locate him. At that moment the gentleman stood up suddenly with an unprecedented sigh of pleasure and voluptuousness. Madam X's coachman suspected what was about to happen and pulled away quickly; nevertheless Madam X felt the impact of the liquid on her face. She looked up, but there wasn't even a cloud in the blue sky. Incomprehensible. She stuck her tongue out and licked delicately.

"Oh!" exclaimed Madam X, falling down, her full weight reclining on the seat, partly from emotion and partly because the coachman had hit a deep pothole that almost caused a shipwreck in the mud.

"Oh!" repeated Madam X, submerged in a white, gelatinous rain. (67)[4]

(—¡P. 5!—gritó, y como respuesta entendió un sonido que no le dejó duda alguna. El caballero se estremecía, doblado en dos; cada vez se agachaba más y Madame X dejó de ver su cabeza. Se puso de pie para intentar localizarla. Y en ese momento el caballero se irguió bruscamente con un gemido inaudito de placer y voluptuosidad. El cochero de Madame X intuyó lo que iba a producirse porque se apartó con velocidad y Madame X recibió un impacto líquido sobre el rostro. Miró hacia arriba, pero ni siquiera había una nube en el cielo límpido. Sacó la lengua y sorbió delicadamente.

—¡Oh!—exclamó Madame X, cayó sentada y se reclinó con todo el peso de su cuerpo sobre los asientos, en parte por la emoción y en parte porque el coche había tomado un profundo bache que casi lo hizo naufragar sobre el barro.

—¡Oh!—repitió Madame X mientras una lluvia gelatinosa y blanca la sumergía.)

Along with the sort of hyperbole that one quickly associates with the conventions of pornography (in this case, the abundant and energetic flow of semen that splashes over Madam X and the indexes of her intense joy of at least having come this close to her objective), this passage turns on the hot pursuit between erotic agent and

---

4. Gambaro, *Lo impenetrable*, 67. All translations are from *The Impenetrable Madam X*, hereafter cited parenthetically in the text.

object, the obstacles to their union, and the displacement of that union in a satisfactory but less than total consumption that leaves the way open for further attempts. While it is true that the relationship between Madam X and El Caballero is initiated by the latter by a letter sent to the woman and sustained by subsequent missives, the man's pursuit of the woman continually backfires (as in the grossly literal detail of this passage). Indeed, it becomes obvious that the pleasure for the man lies in *not* obtaining the woman he approaches, and his instances of ejaculation are always peripheral to the body-to-body consummation that his missives ostensibly imply are his goal. As a consequence, Madam X becomes the furious pursuer of the man: the object becomes the agent of pursuit, which is the inversion on which this passage turns. El Caballero, despite his protestations of ardent desire, constantly eludes her grasp, ejaculates everywhere but where she wants him to, and finally dies on her bedroom floor just as it seems that sexual action is about to occur as she believes it is supposed to in narratives of this kind. While he has awakened lust in Madam X, she can only spur his desire if he does not ever attain her. Like Scheherazade's story, the ending must be constantly displaced if the narrative is to go on and the narrator is to survive. El Caballero's lust only survives to the extent that it is not satisfied, and the narrative about that lust is pursuable only to the extent that desire remains alive, for its decline would abruptly terminate the narrative just as it would abruptly terminate the raison d'être for the relationship between Madam X and El Caballero. His desire is a game of displacement, and erotic displacement (that is, nonfulfillment) is what allows the narrative to exist. Gambaro heads each of her chapters with a miniexcursus about the nature of erotic writing, and one of these epigraphs addresses itself precisely to this paradoxical truth about erotic writing:

> Like eroticism, the erotic novel pursues an impossible goal: "To escape our limits, to go beyond ourselves." Like eroticism, the erotic novel ends up separating what our desire would wish eternally and intimately united: the page and the eye, the reading and the read, the reader and the author. (49)

(La novela erótica, como el erotismo, persigue un fin imposible: "salir de nuestros límites, ir más allá de nosotros mismos".

Como el erotismo, la novela erótica termina por separar lo que nuestro deseo quisiera eterna y estrechamente unido: la página y el ojo, la lectura y lo leído, el lector y el autor.) (51)

By the same token, a perfect erotic union, whether sexual or one of these homologies, destroys the possibility of the text, which can only deal with the absence of that union:

> What conspires against the erotic novel is how the sexual act lacks memory. If memory is called into play, there is no "trance"; if there is no trance, there is no eroticism. As Bataille would put it, "in principle, the erotic experience obliges us to be silent." (116)

> (Lo que conspira contra la novela erótica es la falta de memoria del acto sexual. Si la memoria trabaja, no hay "trance"; si no hay trance, no hay erotismo. Como decía Bataille, "en principio, la experiencia erótica nos compromete al silencio.") (121)

Because *The Impenetrable Madam X* deals with a frustrated erotic union, there is abundant memory of its obstacles and inconclusive encounters, and Gambaro's novel is built around all of the clichés of erotic writing that deal not with the consummation that brings with it the sequence ecstasy–loss of memory–textual silence, but rather precisely with the abundant examples of nonfulfillment, a nonfulfillment that is by El Caballero's design.

However, the novel would soon grow tedious if it were only a facile rewriting of the clichés of its pre-texts, no matter how clever the irony of El Caballero's will to fail in order to remain cloaked by the flames of desire. Gambaro compounds the burlesque of this literature by adopting a vaguely eighteenth-century setting (that century is the source of many of the classics of pornography, beginning with Sade and John Cleland's notorious *Fanny Hill*, 1748–1749). And echoing the erotic adventurism of Laclos's *Les Liaisons dangereuses* (Dangerous Liaisons, 1782) several years before its renewed interest in Christopher Hampton's 1985 play and the subsequent film version, Gambaro organizes her novel in part around an epistolary production that is both bridge and sign of the frustrated encounters between Madam X and El Caballero.

Although Spanish does not allow for the false etymologic conceit of *pen / penis* in a crucial feminist proposal concerning the phallo-centrism of writing and of textual production as a gesture of an aggressive masculinity in which language, like all of the world under the patriarchy, is brought into conformity with male au-thority, it does not take spurious etymology to propose a homology between the wielding of the penis and the wielding of the pen (a homology that includes assorted staffs of authority and the rod of discipline). In Gambaro's novel, the image of what is not penetrable is as much the body as it is language, which is both the medium of expression of the novel and, within it, of Madam X's pursuit of her erotic object; remember that Madam X necessarily becomes the pursuer because El Caballero avoids her to keep his desire alive. To be sure, Madam X wishes to be penetrated by her El Caballero in a conventional sexual transaction; indeed, the novel proposes exaggerated primes of male penetrating (El Caballero's typically hyperbolic member in both size and potency) and female penetrability (Madam X is the caricature of what in Spanish is called *furor uterino* [uterine furor]).

Male and female, therefore, follow a conventional Western scheme, although the novel could well have proposed other se-mantically productive arrangements. Rather, it is in the concept of active/passive or doing/being done where the novel exercises a pattern of realignment, since, although she will be the penetrated female, it is Madam X who is the aggressive doer in obliging El Caballero to comply with her by effecting penetration. It is in her role as the doer that Madam X exercises the pen, wresting from the male realm (a realm where penetrator and doer occupy the same predicative argument slot, rather than the disjunctive slot they occupy in Gambaro's burlesque) the linguistic metonym of his phallic authority. It is by teasing that authority (the role of cock teaser) through textual production in the form of behavior that carefully conforms to the pleas of El Caballero's letters that Madam X is able to execute her agency as the sexual doer. Since it is she who wishes to consummate a sexual union with El Caballero, a sexual union that he in reality evades, she fulfills scrupulously the requests of his letters in the hope that her actions will lead to that union, while he just as scrupulously does not comply with his own instructions, as in the masked ball sequence where Madam X believes she has finally copulated with her elusive lover, only to find out that it was someone else who took advantage of fortuitous circumstances; El Caballero did not even attend the ball for which he gave such careful instructions to Madam X (111–36).

Thus, as the traditional image of the pornographic pursuer, the industrious agent of erotic action, succeeds in setting up obstacle after obstacle that frustrates the union he has proposed and that thereby sustains his ardor, her need to be seduced and to seduce him grows in the face of El Caballero's inability to service the passion he has awakened in Madam X; yet evidence of his potency is abundant. At his death, Madam X is a committed erotomaniac, immediately ready to go off in hot pursuit of another letter-writing suitor as she drags El Caballero's body out of her boudoir.

Gambaro therefore posits two controlling motifs for her novel. One is the burlesque of the pornographic novel's need *not* to consummate too soon the sexual ideal it postulates, to keep the narrative alive through the description of the steps toward and the setbacks surrounding that goal (and this, after all, is only a version of the structure of advances and reversals to be found at the heart of the morphology of all quest literature). The second motif is the inversion of roles brought about by the failure of the ostensible doer (the male) to carry out his program of seduction, resulting in the agentive role being assumed by the customarily passive object/victim in order to attempt to get the job done out of the erotic self-interest that has been awakened in her.

It is Madam X's assumption of the role of doer that provides the feminist dimension to Gambaro's novel. This is so not in the sense of the mere comical inversion of the roles of the doer and the done, nor even in the implied legitimacy of Madam X's erotomania, which is nevertheless a significant break with the conventions of pornography in that the lust of the agent depends on resistance of the object to attain the full erotic investment of the motif of rape on which the pornographic narrative depends for its male-centered interest. Rather, the feminist dimension of *The Impenetrable Madam X* is provided by the commentary of Madam X's reliance on the culmination of her pursuit of El Caballero for sexual fulfillment and on the implied criticism of legitimacy of the simple male-female exchange of the roles of active and passive sexual partners.

This criticism emerges in the figure of Marie, Madam X's servant. Abetting and deceptive servants are also a staple of pornographic fiction. Indeed, the object of pornographic lust may even be a socially inferior individual, as in the case of Cleland's Fanny Hill, whose seducers are invariably of a higher social station. The commonplace of the sexual use of the servant is based on the continuity of exploitation between the domestic servant and the sex slave that animates the conventionalized pornographic imagination and provides multiple versions of the essential narrative action of rape, the apotheosis of nonconsenting abuse inherent in any relationship of demeaning service. However, in line with *The Impenetrable Madam X* as burlesque, Marie is hardly the paradigm of the obsequious servant girl. In fact, she is a shrill critic of her mistress's frantic passion, repeatedly calling her things like "imbecile slut" (imbécil calentona) and "dirty slut" (sucia calentona; 49, 82, 109, 143, 151) that on the one hand describe Madam X's deviation from a conventional upper-class feminine decorum and on the other signal the inappropriateness, even beyond this decorum, of Madam X's assumption of the agentive erotic role.

Marie's imprecations are hardly based on the need of the loyal retainer to protect her foolish mistress, as the gross language adequately indicates, nor are they the consequence of a feminist intuition Gambaro sees instilled among the exploited. Rather, her anger is the consequence of her own erotic self-interest. Marie offers Madam X a lesbian alternative to the latter's frustrated pursuit of El Caballero, and they are actually in bed together when Madam X believes that a letter from a new suitor has arrived for her (150). Committed after all to her heterosexual erotomania (151), she unceremoniously dismisses Marie's attentions for those of a man of her own social class. Pornographic doers belong, of course, to genteel society—this is one of the conventions of the writing—and Marie's earthy views on sex that both denounce Madam X's erotic games and offer an immediately viable alternative to them have nothing to offer the high-born woman for whom the conventions of prestigious cultural texts such as letters of sexual passion have greater allure.

Beneath the texture of burlesque and the comical inversions of pornographic narratives (whose conventions are in reality only confirmed by those inversions, to the extent that the narrative action stays the same, only with redefined agents), Gambaro's *The Impenetrable Madam X* therefore takes on a serious feminist dimension, one that mocks the male-based erotic formulas of sexual conquest that such narratives depend on for their cultural meanings. Yet it seems that Gambaro is unwilling to explore in any depth the lesbian matrix as a legitimate alternative to the unending reenactment, whether by men or by women as the sexual doer, of the pornographic schemata. Marie is dismissed by her mistress and her own sexual availability emerges as nothing more than a shrugged-off commentary from her socially marginal perspective of the stupid games of her social superiors without ever assuming any clear definition as a valid alternative to those games. (To be sure, lesbianism is to be found in pornographic narratives, but only as another form of rape, as are corresponding male homosexual actions: male or female homosexual rape is simply an even higher-pitched version of pornographic sex as the ultimate abyss of the Other.)

The narrative parameters of *The Impenetrable Madam X* are essentially silly, which is part of the originality of a pornographic burlesque by a woman writer. Gambaro's recurring ideological interests are undoubtedly close to the surface in this novel because of the fundamental motifs of exploitation, in sexual terms, involved in the pornographic narrative, even when as a costume drama it involves high-born characters engaging in the libertine pastimes of the wealthy. But this silliness and the dimensions of the costume drama vitiate the serious alternative to the displaced and highly fetishized sexuality (the love letter is an ultimate sexual fetish, as is the pornographic narrative) of courtly passion in the form of no-nonsense sexuality as proffered by Marie. Lesbianism as a radical silencing of the male-focused conventions of pornography lies beyond the scope of the burlesque narrative of *The Impenetrable Madam X*. The novel ends with the parenthetical observation that Marie might not have suspected that she could be the protagonist of a future novel (151), a statement that looks toward the radical repudiation of the pornographic narrative based on lesbianism that Gambaro or any other Argentine author has yet to explore in the serious dimensions that a burlesque like *The Impenetrable Madam X*, in its own perverse way, frustrates. It is not so much that burlesque is inappropriate for exploring alternate sexuality as a corrective for the fossilized schemata of the social text that pornographic narratives rely on for their meaning. Nor is it that Gambaro is to be accused of the inability to "face up" to the challenge of lesbianism, since her drama is hardly characterized by the inability to explore in detail the full destructive dimensions of the social text with which gender remodeling is also concerned. Rather it is simply that the reliance on a structure of simple inversions in *The Impenetrable Madam X* cannot provide for the opportunity for Marie as an alternate sexual sign to play any significant role other than as antiphonic to her mistress's ridiculous erotomania. Another narrative structure will be required for that sign or any other alternative one to emerge with its own fully proposed and articulated social meaning.

CONCLUSIONS

Rather than making conventional use of the space usually destined for summarizing the points that have been made throughout a study, I would instead like to look at three narrative texts that were published in Argentina after the return to constitutional democracy in 1983. Like many of the texts published earlier under the shadows of tyranny, these texts rehearse the sociopolitical and historical parameters of Argentine society that make those shadows an integral part of a recurring national experience and not just a momentary nightmare. That Argentina is once again a society torn by internal conflicts over the legitimacy of institutional power, along with considerable public deception and apathy, lends credibility to the figure of cyclical dictatorships. Yet these works also seek a form of release from the nightmare. This release is not to be found in a jejune optimism that a felicitous conjunction of historical accidents like the drift of events between 1981 (the disastrous Malvinas conflict) and 1983 (the military's retreat to its barracks in humiliation) spells the end to recurring dictatorships. Rather, what is significant about these works—and what is significant about both the sociopolitical commentary that I have discussed and the impressive inventory of creative texts produced in defiance of censorship and other forms of repression between 1976 and 1983—is the lucidity with which they seek to address the ideological constants of Argentine society and to register what opportunities do exist for individuals to work through the constraints

173

of those constants toward a shred of ameliorating decency and dignity in the postmilitary period. It is for this reason that the cultural production of the Proceso must be figured in the tripartite fashion that I have pursued in this study: as the text production of the specific military period (including the importance during this period of earlier contestatorial works like those of Medina and Pizarnik); as the response to these years of military tyranny during the period of redemocratization (the Alfonsín government, 1983–1989); and as the projection that the latter two construals continue to exercise on the most recent writing in Argentina.

By any sensible reckoning, the eight-year period between 1976 and 1983 was the darkest of Argentine national history, not because the stratagems of dictatorship assumed forms different from those of the past but because they were pursued with such unalleviated intensity. There is no need by now to rehearse the grim statistics of the determinedly cynical massacre that took place in the name of Christian family values and the defense of Western traditions. But what Argentine culture since 1983 has found it necessary to do is to record the psychological and spiritual devastation of the military's dirty war and the Proceso de Reorganización Nacional.

Javier Torre, as Director of the Centro Cultural General San Martín in Buenos Aires during the Alfonsín administration, was a major force in the redemocratization of national culture. His novel *Las noches de Maco* (Maco's nights, 1986) is a moving chronicle of this devastation. The protagonist, Maco (a nickname for Marco), is at the center of a process of analysis of the individual who has been a witness to all of the horrendous passages in the tyrannical violation of human rights and dignity at the hands of the self-appointed redeemers of Argentina. A martyr in the etymological sense of the word, Maco's deeply scarred consciousness is a point of reference for a form of collective humiliation than can best be expressed in the mosaic of human detritus that he contemplates in his journey of discovery during the nights of Argentine social history. Maco journeys to the dark side of a world that in his childhood he had known only as a suburban refuge of stern but sincere northern European family love.

Raised in the home of his righteous Irish-Argentine grandmother, Maco grows up within the security of a Catholic, anti-
Peronist environment that is doubly shattered by first the guerrilla
resistance and then the military's dirty war of systematic elimination. *Maco's Nights* is a novel of characters in the sense that, beginning with Maco and moving through a cast of extended family
members who represent an inventory of contemporary Argentine
social issues, the narrative surveys a variety of different individual experiences profoundly affected by the suffering of the period, through the trampling of the innocent, the destruction of
the idealistic, and the deadening corruption of the cynical and the
opportunistic.

It is significant that the secure world of Maco's childhood contains the seeds of its own destruction in the person of the morally
unbending grandmother. At the core of the novel's plot is the
founding event of the shared sexual awakening of Maco and his
cousin Fito, to the horror of their grandmother, who shatters the
homoerotic bond between them in the name of Christian virtue.
Thus, this Castor-Pollux pair becomes a divided identity that is
at the center of Torre's novel. While the one, Fito, becomes a left-
wing Peronist revolutionary and dies horribly at the hands of the
military (the description of his death is one of the most master-
ful passages in recent Argentine fiction), Maco is the bewildered
bystander. He may physically survive the torture and massacre
applied to the more active half of his sociohistoric identity, but like
T. H. White's Claudius, he may outlive the carnage only to turn
over and over in his mind the tragic dimensions for his family.
That it is an immigrant family (but yet not of the paradigmatically
Italian or Jewish majority) that came to Argentina seeking a new
start in life only underscores the microcosmic nature of Maco and
his relations.

Yet Torre does not use a rickety novelistic artifice as a vehicle for
juxtaposing the crosscurrents of recent Argentine history that were
all equally devastated by the Proceso (including the military itself
and whatever claims it may have had to institutional legitimacy).
Rather, his novel elaborates a complex texture of motifs based on

Maco's nuclear experiences, complemented by those of the other characters whose destruction he witnesses. By seeking the roots of the Proceso in the underlying structures of national identity, by chronicling the key experiences in this collective tragedy, and by focusing on one individual consciousness as the synthesis of the suffering of an entire society, Torre has produced an emblematic text of the literature of a redemocratized Argentina.

Of the contemporary Argentine novelists, Reina Roffé provides perhaps the best example of analytical narrative writing that explores the nuances and shadings of the human consciousness and its various strategies of self-reflection and representation. Although her works all deal with female characters, her fictional discourse is specifically feminine not because it deals with the experiences of women, but because it constitutes the attempt to break down fossilized narrative modes that enclose symbolic representation rather than exposing it to the multiplicity of divergent signifiers urgently necessary to ensure an adequate sense of the complex human experience.

Those barriers begin with the distinctions between life and literature, living and representation, an experiential "I" and a narratively symbolic "I," and the solipsism of the individual enmeshed in her own disturbing encounters with the world and the various ways in which knowledge about such encounters may be objectified via the forms of symbolic representation under the guide of second- and third-person pronouns that install the sensation of reality beyond one's personal mind and body. If the novel is the meeting ground for such attempts at semiotic objectification, to the extent that it is a network of strategies of symbolic representation, beginning with basic constituent elements and building through situation and plot toward a hegemonic inscription of life, it is also the locus for the multiple problematics of the reading, interpretation, and (re)writing codes of knowledge and expression.

The protagonist of Roffé's *La rompiente* (The reef, 1987) is a woman who sallies forth from the enclosure, literal and metaphoric, of the self, to collide with the breakers of existence on its most trivial level. At the same time, she narrates herself in the ensnaring containment of the text, which promises to tell her what the substance and quality of her experiences are but which in fact only serves to further fragment them with the slippage of narrative representation. As a consequence, the novel presents a highly refracted image of the individual (the motif of "through a glass darkly"), while in the process it plays on all of the disruptional (from the point of view of a schematic ideal of inscribed representation) details of multiple narrative voices—the deictic disjunction of "I" versus "you," life as metafiction, and the frustration of plot experiences.

The Reef, it must be noted, is hardly an example of the so-called self-contained novel that only seems to be narrating the act of narration. Rather, the metafictional qualities of Roffé's novel are part of a self-reflective discourse that is concerned directly with the textual representation of a particular form of human experience (roughly, the Everywoman in a hostile and destructive environment signaled by the literal fact of sociopolitical exile). And the forms of the textualization of this experience involve a sure and firm manipulation of a feminine discourse that lay bare the disquieting, disturbing qualities of that experience beyond facile promises of a newly reconstituted social world. As Gimbernat has demonstrated, there is a significant emergence of women's writing as part of the cultural production grounded in the Proceso. This is not only because the period in general terms corresponds to the impressive development of feminist agendas internationally but also more specifically because of the degradation of women's culture that is an integral part of all-male, patriarchal, and hierarchical military institutions, especially as they are defended as the basis of national identity. Both the feminine and the feminized (most specifically but not exclusively, sexual subalternities) either get short shrift or, alternatively, they are overdetermined by the ideology of military tyranny, and it was inevitable that women's writing would become an important site of countercultural production, which is why it has figured so prominently in this study.

The core of Enrique Medina's collection of short stories, *Desde un mundo civilizado* (From a civilized world, 1987) are a series of microtexts, a form of brief narrative frequent in Latin America (Borges produced some notable examples), and they are in the first instance the result of having been written for the confined space of the newspaper column. Indeed, the first feature these texts reveal is a continuity or intertextuality with the news items on violent crimes, personal tragedies, and collective disasters that are the mainstay of the daily newspaper. Echoing the tenet that we inhabit a civilized world from which such events are regrettable deviations, Medina explores how they are quite to the contrary exemplary vignettes of a society in which the individual is constantly at the mercy of a dynamic of structural violence that masks itself with the illusion of civility and law and order.

It is notable that Medina, who has established his reputation on the basis of unflinching (and the not unproblematic) portrayal of the oppression of individuals as a consequence of the abiding social disorders of their native Argentina, continues the expanded perspective he inaugurated in *Año nuevo en Nueva York* (New year in New York, 1986) to include narratives datelined in other parts of the "civilized world" (for example, "El coyote," which deals with the death in the American desert of illegal Mexican immigrants abandoned by their paid guide or *coyote*, and "El émbolo" [embolism] on the practice of carrying out capital punishment by lethal injection). In terms of the need in Argentina both to denounce a national structural violence that made military tyranny possible and even welcome, and to overcome the tendency for a country that has emerged from a recent past like Argentina's to view itself as a pariah among self-reputedly civilized nations, *From a Civilized World* exemplifies the writing of contemporary Argentina that for the past seven years has attempted to redefine a national consciousness on the basis of an analysis of sociocultural dynamics that is broader than the denunciatory testimonial. Since many of these texts deal directly or by implication with recent actual events that have appeared on the front pages of the newspaper, Medina is also demonstrating the ability of literary narrative to provide a more probing inquiry into the motivations and consequences to the individual of acts and events that journalism can only chronicle.

Specifically, Medina frequently focuses on the interior processes of the so-called agents of violence to suggest their compulsions as well as to portray how they are affected psychologically by their actions.

Another notable feature of Medina's collection is the decision to dedicate each one of the thirty-six texts to a group of individuals with whom he as a writer identifies. The result is the evocation of a broad network of men and women (and children) with a shared commitment to knowing how the world is hardly a civilized place, but yet by extension how such knowledge can contribute to the forging of a decent society. This is, after all, the global context of all of the writing that has been examined in this study.

CHRONOLOGY

1966

Murder of trade union members (Rosendo García), increase in strikes, violent university student protests. Dismissal of President Arturo Illia (June 28) and seizure of power by a military junta that designates itself as the Revolución Argentina and immediately dissolves the National Congress, the provincial legislatures, and political parties. Lieutenant General Juan Carlos Onganía assumes command as president. The end of university autonomy, and the beginning of a process of cultural censorship "for the protection" of public morals and an economic program inspired by extensive free trade.

1967

Meeting of the III Conferencia Extraordinaria del Consejo Interamericano Económico y Social (Extraordinary Conference of the Inter-American Economic and Social Council), organization of the OAS (Organization of American States) and postponement of its final deliberations until the presidential meeting in Punta del Este, Uruguay, with the attendance of President Lyndon Johnson. Conflicts with the CGT (Confederación General del Trabajo [General Labor Confederation]) and suspension of the personnel of various labor unions, with the control of the funds of some of them; salary freezes. Diverse reactions to papal encyclical Populorum Progressio, concerning the relationship of Catholics with the world crises.

Assassination of Che Guevara in Bolivia (October 8). In Washington the opera *Bomarzo* opens, with libretto by Manuel Mujica Láinez and music by Alberto Ginastera; it had previously been banned in the Teatro Colón by the Onganía government.

1968

Meeting of Onganía with 180 functionaries and officials of the armed forces to analyze and extend the operations of the Revolución Argentina, followed by the resignation of many of these officials. Division of the CGT into CGT de los Argentinos and CGT Azopardo. Union criticism and clashes toward the Revolución Argentina are accentuated. Pope Paul VI attends the XXXIX Congreso Eucarístico International (International Eucharistic Conference), held in Bogotá. A state of siege is declared in the Barrio Latino of Paris in response to the aggressiveness of the student demonstrations, followed by general and national strikes. Leopoldo Torre Nilsson premieres *Martín Fierro,* and Fernando Solanas is lauded in Italy for his film *La hora de los hornos* (The hour of the furnaces).

1969

Onganía attempts to reach a social and economic agreement with 140 business leaders to stave off price increases. Uprising in Córdoba (the Cordobazo) and rapid repercussion in the interior of the country, with many victims and enormous loss of "material goods." Onganía attributes the labor uprisings to "an organized extremist force 'group.' " Resignation of his entire cabinet, governors, and high-level functionaries. Assassination by unknown persons of Augusto Vandor, union leader and secretary general of the UOM (Unión Obrera Metalúrgica [Metallurgy Worker's Union]). Implementation of a state of siege to stem the wave of assassination attempts. Intervention of the CGT.

1970

A new currency is introduced. Guerrilla action increases (seizure of La Calera, Garín, etc.) and terrorist operations intensify, along with attacks on and abductions of commercial planes. Kidnapping and assassination of Pedro Eugenio Aramburu, former president of the Revolución Libertadora government that had overthrown Perón, by the commando Juan José Valle of the Montoneros guerrilla group. The death penalty is implemented for those guilty of terrorist acts and kidnapping. The Junta de Comandantes en Jefe (The joint chief of staff) of the Armed Forces depose Onganía and govern for several days, until the naming of Brigadier General Roberto Marcelo Levingston as president. Convention of the CGT Azopardo and naming of José Ignacio Rucci as secretary general. Numerous political parties, convened by the personal delegate of Perón, Jorge Daniel Paladino, form a front called La Hora del Pueblo (The Hour of the People). Urban guerrilla warfare becomes internationalized in Latin America. Salvador Allende wins the Chilean presidential elections, installing the first Marxist government in America elected at the polls. Awarding of the Nobel Prize in Chemistry to the Argentine Luis Federico Leloir.

1971

Levingston pushes for multiparty political unity and a national development program. Rucci warns the government that the CGT will not accept salary cuts, while from Madrid Perón threatens to "bring down the dictatorship." General Lanusse introduces the principles of the Gran Acuerdo Nacional (Great National Accord) and dissension begins within the military ranks. General strikes increase and street demonstrations continue with police confrontations occurring throughout the nation. Overthrow of Levingston; Lanusse assumes the presidency. Political activity resumes, while leaders increasingly travel to Madrid for interviews with Perón. Lanusse meets with Allende in Salta, producing something of an ideological opening that will culminate with the announcement of free elections for March 11, 1973, anticipating the cession of power on May 25 of that same year. Cámpora replaces Paladino as personal representative of Perón, while Isabel Perón visits Argentina to solve the internal problems of Peronismo before the upcoming elections.

1972

Trips to Spain by politicians and union leaders continue. The Justicialista (Peronista) party achieves official recognition and a mansion in Olivos for Perón to reside in upon returning from exile. Lanusse admits that the features of the Gran Acuerdo Nacional imply a democratic and constitutional process for the nation, but he sets conditions for programs, and candidates must be approved by the ruling elite of the armed forces. The ban on Perón is lifted, and he returns to Argentina to form a political coalition of parties under the name of the Frente Justicialista de Liberación (Justicialista Liberation Front). Elections are confirmed for March 11, 1973, and Perón returns to Madrid after rejecting the presidential nomination.

1973

National elections are held, with the triumph of Héctor Cámpora and Vicente Solano Lima, who assume their offices on May 25. An amnesty law is signed, freeing all political prisoners. At the same time repressive legislation is repealed. A Social Pact is signed between the CGT and the CGE (Confederación General Económica) by which salaries undergo large increases and mandatory labor arbitration is suspended for two years. Perón returns to Argentina with Isabel, and armed confrontations take place on the highway to Ezeiza International Airport, resulting in many wounded and dead. Perón lands at the Morón military base and begins to take charge of his campaign for the presidency, following the resignation of Cámpora and Solano Lima. After a brief period in which the presidency is covered by Raúl Lastiri, the Perón-Perón team gives the aging General his third mandate, while for the first time a woman becomes vice president of Argentina. Terrorism, however, worsens, and the armed forces, following the assassination and abduction of high-ranking military leaders, demand that violence be fought. Various military operations are organized against subversion and terrorism. The secretary of the CGT, José Rucci, is murdered, and Salvador Allende is killed in Chile following a military rebellion that places General Augusto Pinochet in power.

1974

Perón exhorts the people to adopt measures to avoid the waste of energy and resources. In the celebration for May 1, Perón confronts the established leftist groups that operated within Peronism. Terrorist acts, assassinations, and abductions continue against civilians and the military. Perón dies on July 1 and Isabel assumes the presidency. The ultraright extremist organization AAA (Asociación Anticomunista Argentina) appears on the scene and joins the wave of terror. Several companies are nationalized and José López Rega, as Minister of Government, arranges for the return of the remains of Eva Perón on November 16.

1975

Union conflicts increase throughout the nation, and even farming strikes occur. Violence from the left and from the right increase, including attacks, hijackings, and assaults on military units, with the one on the 29th Regiment of Formosa being the most serious. Inflation rises day by day, conflicts between the CGT and Peronism insiders become more and more serious along with numerous absences of the president, either for rest or illness. Italo Luder momentarily assumes the presidency. Political sectors warn against the situation. A military uprising against the government is stifled. Labor incidents and pillaging generate great instability in various provinces; the president signs a decree that authorizes the military to intervene in Tucumán against terrorist forces, especially the ERP (Ejército Revolucionario del Pueblo [Revolutionary Army of the People]). Political arrests are noticeably numerous.

1976

The year begins with a situation of generalized crisis. The president goes through thirty-two ministers in one and one-half years. Criticism and oppositional stances appear within Peronism. Extremist activity, in spite of the thirty-two encampments that the army claims to have wiped out, continues, from the left as well as from the right. Union conflicts grow also and items of primary need begin to become scarce. Despite the wages pacts enacted by the executive power, it is this same power that increases salary raises in violation of its own agreements. Business and military sectors begin to mobilize against the executive power. Isabel Perón refuses to resign, although she claims to have no intention of presenting herself as a candidate in the elections planned for December 12. General labor standstill and sectorial strikes occur with growing frequency. On March 24 the armed forces detain the president and take power; General Jorge Rafael Videla accedes to the first magistracy. He dissolves Parliament, removes the members of the Supreme Court, prohibits all types of political and union activity, suspends the right to strike, etc. The Minister of Economy, José Alfredo Martínez de Hoz, increases fuel costs, establishes a new monetary order, decrees new taxation measures, and frees prices. Videla, for his part, prohibits the publication of news about abductions and assassinations of terrorist origin. The CGT is taken over by the government, which announces it will attack subversion until achieving its total elimination. Sanctions are brought against political leaders who are then removed from office and imprisoned.

1977

The annual inflation index begins to increase. The United States issues a report conveying the violation of human rights on the part of the Argentine government; the Argentine government warns the government in Washington that it will not permit foreign interference in national matters. The conflict over the Beagle channel between Chile and Argentina comes to an end. Various labor confederations are dissolved. Videla meets privately in Washington with President Carter, whom he informs that the fight against subversion is coming to an end. The "Gravier Group" is accused of diverting funds to subsidize subversive groups.

1978

Diplomatic relations with Chile worsen, and Argentina rejects British arbitration. Subsequently, the intervention of the Holy See is sought to mediate between the two South American nations. An outcry occurs when the North American bank Export-Import (Exibank) refuses to grant credit to finance the Yaciretá hydroelectric project, alleging a growing violation of human rights by the Argentine government. Several politicians including Ricardo Balbín and diverse party leaders solicit the repeal of the state of siege and the revision of the economic plan, as well as the normalization of political, union, and business activities. Argentina's victory in the World Soccer Cup generates an unprecedented state of public euphoria. The King and Queen of Spain visit Argentina, accompanied by scandal over the theft of Queen Sofia's stole.

1979

Negotiations with the Holy See continue over the Beagle conflict. David Rockefeller, as president of Chase Manhattan Bank, arrives in Buenos Aires and suggests ways to address the problem of inflation. State-owned companies begin to be privatized. The XXXIX Asamblea Ordinaria del Episcopado Latinoamericano (Ordinary Assembly of Latin American Bishops) meets, and various texts on the Puebla document are circulated. At the same time ecclesiastic members visit President Videla and express to him their concern for the large number of disappeared persons and political prisoners, as well as for the distressing economic situation. The Inter-American Commission on Human Rights visits prisons and interviews various individuals and family members of detained and disappeared persons. Former President Héctor J. Cámpora—housed up to this point in the Mexican Embassy—is allowed to leave Argentina due to serious illness. Downfall of the dictatorship of Somoza in Nicaragua and that of the Salvadoran colonels. John Paul II visits Mexico, Poland, and the United States.

1980

The cost of living continues to rise and with it, inflation. The Argentine government refuses to participate in the embargo of grain to the Soviet Union proposed by the United States in retaliation for the invasion of Afghanistan, which is also repudiated by the Argentine government. Closure of important financial and banking firms occur, extreme temperatures necessitate the suspension of classes and there is unprecedented flooding all around Buenos Aires. The law of Asociaciones Gremiales is established and unions are authorized to keep separate account of the funds for social works. The report prepared by the Inter-American Commission on Human Rights is circulated, and it includes serious criticisms of the Argentine situation; the report is rejected by the Argentine government, which adduces "major defects" in it. Dialogues between the military junta and political leaders commence, but without any hope for elections. The president of Brazil visits Argentina and is repaid with a trip to his country by General Videla. The military junta arranges for the replacement of Videla by Lieutenant General Roberto Eduardo Viola as president. The public is moved by the granting of the Nobel Peace Prize to Adolfo Pérez Esquivel for his militancy in defense of human rights. Somoza is assassinated in Paraguay, and Carter is replaced as president of the United States by Ronald Reagan.

1981

With internal violence under the control of the military, an ideological offensive is mounted. The process of censorship and cultural control is stepped up. A law governing radio broadcasting is specified, which includes, among other things, the criteria of morality, defense of the family, and of the need to halt corruption. Strict sanctions are imposed with the doctrine of National Security passed by the National Congress and signed into law by the Executive Power on September 28, 1974. In Buenos Aires a theatrical experiment emerges called Teatro Abierto, bringing together hundreds of actors and dramatists and attracting a large public following. The theater in which the cycle of plays was to be performed is burned to the ground, and the program continues at another locale. In November Lieutenant General Viola relinquishes his duties, and after a brief substitution by General Horacio T. Liendo, Lieutenant General Leopoldo Fortunato Galtieri assumes the presidency.

1982

On April 2 the invasion of the Malvinas takes place, as an action against the British occupation; on June 18, as a result of the defeat of the Argentine troops, President Galtieri "voluntarily retires," being replaced—following a brief interim government under Alfredo Saint Jean—by General Reynaldo Benito Bignone. Very restrictive norms are established for public information concerning the Malvinas conflict, the disappeared, and the Mothers of the Plaza de Mayo. In February, the Episcopate calls attention to the increase of "immorality in the media." Complaints continue against the blacklists of actors and journalists, the confiscation of editions of books and magazines, and movie censorship. In March the CGT and sixty-two other organizations call a general work stoppage. The second cycle of Teatro Abierto takes place.

1983

President Bignone calls a meeting of the unaligned nations in New Delhi. Telephone threats continue against writers and radio and television reporters, some of whom suffer intimidating acts such as kidnapping. The book by the French author Jean Pierre Bousquet, *Las locas de Plaza de Mayo* (The mad women of Plaza de Mayo), appears after serious problems with the publishing house. In November censorship is officially suspended. On December 10, before the National Congress, Raúl Alfonsín is sworn in as constitutional president of Argentina.

1984

Trials initiated by the national government begin against the military leaders; the armed forces are offered the chance to judge themselves in accordance with a law that invests the Supreme Council of the Armed Forces with the right to try its own members. The National Commission for the Investigation of Human Rights is established and is presided over by the writer Ernesto Sabato, who will author a report known afterwards by the title, *Nunca más* (Never more).

1989

Peronista president Carlos Menem, in the spirit of *punto final* (closing the books), pardons most of the principal military officials found guilty of human rights abuses and violations of the constitution.

REFERENCES

(Items marked by an asterisk represent the original sources of material included in this volume.)

Acevedo, Zelmar. *Homosexualidad: hacia la destrucción de los mitos.* Buenos Aires: Ediciones del Ser, 1985.

Agosin, Marjorie. *Circles of Madness: Mothers of the Plaza de Mayo.* Translated by Celeste Kostopulus-Cooperman. Fredonia, N.Y.: White Pine Press, 1992.

Aguinis, Marcos. *Carta esperanzada a un general; puente sobre el abismo.* Buenos Aires: Sudamericana/Planeta, 1983. A fragment, "Hopeful Letter to a General: A Fragment," translated by David William Foster, appeared in the special issue on Latin America of *Massachusetts Review* 27, nos. 3–4 (1988): 712–21.

Anderson, Martin Edwin. *Dossier Secreto: Argentina's Desaparecidos and the Myth of the "Dirty War."* Boulder, Colo.: Westview Press, 1993.

Argentina. Comisión Nacional sobre la Desaparición de Personas. *Nunca más.* Buenos Aires: EUDEBA, 1984. Published also in English, with an introduction by Ronald Dworkin. New York: Farrar Straus Giroux, in association with Index on Censorship, London, 1986.

"Argentina: 1955–1989." Special issue of *Los ensayistas* 26–27 (1989).

Avellaneda, Andrés. *Censura, autoritarismo y cultura: Argentina 1960–1983.* 2 vols. Buenos Aires: Centro Editor de América Latina, 1986.

———. *El tema del peronismo en la narrativa argentina.* Ph.D. diss., University of Illinois, 1973. Published in a substantially revised edition as *El habla de la ideología: modos de réplica literaria en la Argentina contemporánea.* Buenos Aires: Editorial Sudamericana, 1983.

Bazán, Juan. "Enrique Medina." In *Narrativa paraguaya y latinoamericana,* 259–73. Asunción, 1976.

Birkmoe, Diane S. "The Virile Voice of Marta Lynch." *Revista de estudios hispánicos* 16, no. 2 (1982): 191–211.

Bixler, Jacqueline Eyring. "Games and Reality on the Latin American Stage." *Latin American Literary Review* 24 (1984): 22–35.

Blanco Amores de Pagella, Angela. "Manifestaciones del teatro del absurdo en Argentina." *Latin American Theatre Review* 8, no. 1 (1974): 21–24.

Bonasso, Miguel. *Recuerdo de la muerte.* Buenos Aires: Editorial Bruguera Argentina, 1984.

Brownmiller, Susan. *Against Our Will: Men, Women and Rape.* New York: Simon and Schuster, 1975.

Bürger, Peter. *Teoría de la vanguardia,* trans. Jorge García. Barcelona: Península, 1987.

Camps, Ramón J. A. *Caso Timerman: punto final.* Buenos Aires: Tribuna Abierta, 1982.

Carballido, Emilio. "Griselda Gambaro o modos de hacernos pensar en la manzana." *Revista iberoamericana* 73 (1970): 629–34.

Cardoso, O. R., R. Kirschbaum, and E. van der Kooy. *Malvinas, la trama secreta.* 13th ed. Buenos Aires: Sudamericana/Planeta, 1984. Published in English as *Falklands, the Secret Plot,* trans. Bernard Ethell. East Moseley, Surrey, England: Preston Editions, 1987.

Carter, Angela. *The Sadeian Woman and the Ideology of Pornography.* New York: Pantheon Books, 1978.

Cesareo, Mario. "Cuerpo humano e historia en la novela del Proceso." In *Fascismo y experiencia literaria: reflexiones para una recanonización,* edited by Hernán Vidal, 501–31. Minneapolis: Institute for the Study of Ideologies and Literature, 1985.

Charney, Maurice. *Sexual Fiction.* London: Methuen, 1981.

Corradi, Juan E., Patricia Weiss Fagen, and Manuel Antonio Garretón. *Fear at the Edge: State Terror and Resistance in Latin America.* Berkeley: University of California Press, 1992.

Cortázar, Julio. *Argentina: años de alambradas culturales.* Edición a cargo de Saúl Yurkievich. Buenos Aires: Muchnik Editores, 1984.

Cypess, Sandra Messinger. "Physical Imagery in the Works of Griselda Gambaro." *Modern Drama* 8 (1975): 357–64.

———. "The Plays of Griselda Gambaro." In *Dramatists in Revolt: The New Latin American Theater*, compiled by Leon F. Lyday and George W. Woodyard, 95–109. Austin: University of Texas Press, 1976.

Daly, Mary. *Gyn/ecology: The Metaethics of Radical Feminism.* Boston: Beacon Press, 1978.

Deutsch, Sandra McGee, and Ronald H. Dolkart, eds. *The Argentine Right: Its History and Intellectual Origins, 1910 to the Present.* Washington, D.C.: SR Books, 1993.

Didion, Joan. *Salvador.* New York: Simon and Schuster, 1983.

Driskell, Charles B. "Theatre in Buenos Aires: 1976–1977." *Latin American Theatre Review* 11, no. 2 (1978): 103–10.

Duhalde, Eduardo Luis. *El estado terrorista argentino.* Buenos Aires: Ediciones El Caballito, 1983.

Dworkin, Andrea. *Intercourse.* New York: The Free Press, 1987.

Eagleton, Terry. *Literary Theory: An Introduction.* Minneapolis: University of Minnesota Press, 1983.

Etchepareborda, Roberto. "La bibliografía reciente sobre la cuestión Malvinas (primera parte)." *Revista interamericana de bibliografía* 34, no. 1 (1984): 1–52; 34, no. 2 (1984): 227–88.

Feijóo, María del Carmo. "The Challenge of Constructing Civilian Peace." In *The Women's Movement in Latin America: Feminism and the Transition to Democracy*, edited by Jane S. Jaquette, 72–94. Boston: Unwin Hyman, 1989.

Femenía, Nora A. "Argentina's Mothers of Plaza de Mayo: The Mourning Process from Junta to Democracy." *Feminist Studies* 13 (1987): 9–18.

Ficción y política: la narrativa Argentina durante el proceso militar. Buenos Aires: Alianza Editorial; Minneapolis: Institute for the Study of Ideologies and Literature, 1987.

Fisher, Jo. *Mothers of the Disappeared.* London: Zed Books; Boston: South End Press, 1987.

Foster, David William. *Alternate Voices in the Latin American Narrative.* Columbia: University of Missouri Press, 1985.

*———. "Argentine Sociopolitical Commentary, the Malvinas Conflict, and Beyond: Rhetoricizing a National Experience." *Latin American Research Review* 22, no. 1 (1987): 7–34.

———. *Currents in the Contemporary Argentine Novel.* Columbia: University of Missouri Press, 1975.

———. "Entrevista con Enrique Medina sobre su nueva novela, *Con el trapo en la boca.*" *Chasqui* 13, nos. 2–3 (1984): 67–79.

———. *From Mafalda to Los Supermachos: Latin American Graphic Humor as Popular Culture.* Boulder, Colo.: Lynne Rienner, 1989.

———. *Gay and Lesbian Themes in Latin American Writing.* Austin: University of Texas Press, 1991. A fragment appeared as "The Search for Text: Some Examples of Latin American Gay Writing." *Ibero-Amerikanisches Archiv* neue folge 14, no. 3 (1988): 329–56.

*———. "Identidades polimórficas y planteo metateatral en *Extraño juguete* de Susana Torres Molina." *Alba de América* 7, nos. 12–13 (1989): 75–86.

———. "Imagining Argentine Socio-Political History in Some Recent American Novels." *Yearbook of Comparative and General Literature* 39 (1990–1991 [i.e., 1993]): 75–86.

*———. "Introduction." In Enrique Medina, *Las tumbas (The Tombs),* v–xiii, trans. David William Foster. New York: Garland, 1993.

———. "Latin American Documentary Narrative." *PMLA* 99 (1984), 41–55.

———. "El lenguaje como vehículo espiritual en *Los siameses* de Griselda Gambaro." *Escritura* 8 (1979): 241–57.

———. "The Manipulation of the Horizons of Reader Expectation in Two Examples of Argentine Lesbian Writing: Discourse Power and Alternate Sexuality." In *Spanish and Portuguese Distinguished Lecture Series: Selected Texts,* 117–27. Boulder: University of Colorado, Department of Spanish and Portuguese; Society of Spanish and Spanish-American Studies, 1989.

———. "Marta Lynch: The Individual and the Argentine Political Process." *Latin American Digest* 10, no. 1 (1976): 11, 19–20.

*———. "Narrativa testimonial Argentina durante los años del 'Proceso.'" In *Testimonio y literatura,* edited by René Jara and Hernán Vidal, 138–54. Minneapolis: Institute for the Study of Ideologies and Literature; Society for the Study of Contemporary Hispanic and Lusophone Revolutionary Literatures, 1986. Originally as "Narrativa testimonial argentina en los años del 'Proceso.'" *Plural* 2a época 150 (1984): 21–23.

*———. "Los parámetros de la narrativa argentina durante el 'Proceso de Reorganización Nacional.'" In *Ficción y política: la narrativa*

argentina durante el proceso militar, edited by Beatriz Sarlo, 96–108. Buenos Aires: Alianza Editorial; Minneapolis: Institute for the Study of Ideologies and Literature, 1987. Also *Letras* [Curitiba] 37 (1988): 152–67.

———. "Paschal Symbology in Echeverría's *El matadero.*" *Studies in Short Fiction* 7 (1970): 257–63.

*———. "Pornography and the Feminine Erotic: Griselda Gambaro's *Lo impenetrable.*" *Monographic Review/Revista monográfica* 7 (1991): 284–96.

*———. "Raping Argentina: Marta Lynch's *Informe bajo llave.*" *Centennial Review* 25, no. 3 (1991): 663–80. Also as "Violando Argentina: *Informe bajo llave* de Marta Lynch." *Letras* [Curitiba] 39 (1990): 95–113.

———. Preface to *The Redemocratization of Argentine Culture, 1983 and Beyond: An International Research Symposium,* edited by David William Foster, 1–6. Tempe: Arizona State University, Center for Latin American Studies, 1989.

———. "The Representation of the Body in the Poetry of Alejandra Pizarnik," *Hispanic Review* 62, no. 3 (1994): 319–47.

———. "Semantic Relativity in Ricardo Monti's *La visita.*" *American Hispanist* 34–35 (1979 [i.e., 1981]): 17–20.

———. *Social Realism in the Argentine Narrative.* Chapel Hill: University of North Carolina Studies in the Romance Languages and Literatures, 1986.

———. "The Texture of Dramatic Action in the Plays of Griselda Gambaro." *Hispanic Journal* 1, no. 2 (1980): 57–66.

*———. "Traspasando los géneros literarios." *Ideas '92* 2, no. 1 (1988): 83–88.

Foucault, Michel. *Discipline and Punish: The Birth of the Prison.* Translated by Alan Sheridan. New York: Pantheon Books, 1977.

Franco, Jean. "Gender, Death and Resistance: Facing the Ethical Vacuum." *Chicago Review* 35, no. 4 (1987): 59–79. Also in *Fear at the Edge: State Terror and Resistance in Latin America,* edited by Juan E. Corradi et al., 104–18. Berkeley: University of California Press, 1992.

———. "Self-Destructing Heroines." *Minnesota Review* 22 (1984): 105–15.

———. "Women, Feminism, and the Transition to Democracy in Latin America." In *Latin American and Caribbean Contemporary Record,* ed. Abraham F. Lowenthal, A43-A62. New York: Holmes and Meier, 1988.

Frontalini, Daniel, and María Cristina Caiati. *El mito de la guerra sucia.* Buenos Aires: Centro de Estudios Legales y Sociales, 1984.

Gabetta, Carlos. *Todos somos subversivos.* Buenos Aires: Editorial Bruguera Argentina, 1983. Originally published in French in 1979.

Gallop, Jane. *Thinking through the Body.* New York: Columbia University Press, 1988.

Gambaro, Griselda. *Lo impenetrable.* Buenos Aires: Torres Agüero Editor, 1984. English version as *The Impenetrable Madam X.* Translated by Evelyn Picon Garfield. Detroit: Wayne State University Press, 1991.

———. *Teatro 1: Real envido; La malasangre; Del sol naciente.* Buenos Aires: Ediciones de la Flor, 1984. *La malasangre,* 57–110.

Giella, Miguel Angel, Peter Roster, and Leandro Urbina. "Entrevista Griselda Gambaro: la ética de la confrontación." In *Teatro: Nada que ver. Sucede lo que pasa,* Griselda Gambaro, 7–37. Ottawa: Girol Books, 1983.

Gimbernat González, Ester. *Aventuras del desacuerdo: novelistas argentinas de los 80.* Buenos Aires: Danilo Alberto Vergara, 1992.

———. "Entrevista." *Hispamerica* 40 (1985): 35–42.

Graziano, Frank. *Divine Violence: Spectacle, Psychosexuality, and Radical Christianity in the Argentine "Dirty War."* Boulder, Colo.: Westview Press, 1992.

Gregorich, Luis. "La literatura dividida." In *Represión y reconstrucción de una cultura: el caso argentino,* compiled by Saúl Sosnowski, 121–24. Buenos Aires: Editorial Universitaria de Buenos Aires, 1988.

Greimas, A. J., and J. Courtés. *Semiotics and Language: An Analytical Dictionary.* Translated by Larry Crist et al. Bloomington: Indiana University Press, 1982.

Griffin, Susan. *Pornography and Silence: Culture's Revenge against Nature.* New York: Harper and Row, 1981.

Gubar, Susan, and Joan Hoff, eds. *For Adult Users Only: The Dilemma of Violent Pornography.* Bloomington: Indiana University Press, 1989.

Guest, Iain. *Behind the Disappearances: Argentina's Dirty War against Human Rights and the United Nations.* Philadelphia: University of Pennsylvania Press, 1990.

Hodges, Donald C. *Argentina's "Dirty War": An Intellectual Biography.* Austin: University of Texas Press, 1991.

Holzapfel, Tamara. "Griselda Gambaro's Theatre of the Absurd." *Latin American Theatre Review* 4, no. 1 (1971): 5–11.

Jameson, Fredric. "Criticism in History." In *The Ideologies of Theory: Essays 1971–1986*, 1:119–36. Minneapolis: University of Minnesota Press, 1988.

———. "Pleasure: A Political Issue." In *Formations of Pleasure*, 1–14. London: Routledge and Kegan Paul, 1983.

———. *The Political Unconscious: Narrative as a Socially Symbolic Act.* Ithaca, N.Y.: Cornell University Press, 1981.

Jara, René. *Los límites de la representación: la novela chilena del golpe.* Madrid: Fundación Instituto Shakespeare, Instituto de Cine y Radio-Televisión, 1985.

Jozef, Bella. "Enrique Medina, o tempo sem recuperação." In *O jogo mágico*, 118–20. Rio de Janeiro: Livraria José Olympio Editora, 1980.

Kaiser-Lenoir, Claudia. *El grotesco criollo: estilo teatral de una época.* La Habana: Casa de las Américas, 1977.

Kaminsky, Amy K. *Reading the Body Politic: Feminist Criticism and Latin American Women Writers.* Minneapolis: University of Minnesota Press, 1993.

Kendrick, Walter M. *The Secret Museum: The History of Pornography in Literature.* New York: Viking, 1987.

Kon, Daniel. *Los chicos de la guerra; hablan los soldados que estuvieron en las Malvinas.* 8th ed. Buenos Aires: Editorial Galerna, 1983.

Kovadloff, Santiago. *Argentina, oscuro país; ensayos sobre un tiempo de quebranto.* Buenos Aires: Torres Agüero, 1983.

———. *Una cultura de catacumbas y otros ensayos.* Buenos Aires: Botella al Mar, 1982.

———. *Por un futuro imperfecto; ensayos.* Buenos Aires: Botella al Mar, 1987.

Larsen, Neil. "Sport as Civil Society: The Argentinean Junta Plays Championship Soccer." In *Discourse of Power: Culture, Hegemony and the Authoritarian State*, edited by Neil Larsen. Minneapolis: Institute for the Study of Ideologies and Literature, 1983.

Lavandera, Beatriz R. "Hacia una tipología del discurso autoritario." *Plural* [Buenos Aires] 1 (1985): 26–35.

Lindstrom, Naomi. "Women's Discourse Difficulties in a Novel by Marta Lynch [La señora Ordóñez]." *Ideologies and Literature* 4, no. 17 (1983): 339–48.

————. *Women's Voice in Latin American Literature.* Washington, D.C.: Three Continents Press, 1989.

Lynch, Marta. *Informe bajo llave.* Buenos Aires: Editorial Sudamericana, 1983.

————. *La penúltima versión de la Colorada Villanueva.* 4th ed. Buenos Aires: Editorial Sudamericana, 1979.

Mantega, Guido. "Sexo e poder nas sociedades autoritárias: a face erótica da dominação." In *Sexo e poder,* compiled by Guido Mantega, 9–34. São Paulo: Editora Brasiliense, 1979.

Martini Real, Juan. *La vida entera.* Barcelona: Bruguera, 1981.

Masiello, Francine. "La Argentina durante el Proceso: las múltiples resistencias de la cultura." In *Ficción y política: la narrativa argentina durante el proceso militar,* 11–29. Buenos Aires: Alianza Editorial; Minneapolis: Institute for the Study of Ideologies and Literature, 1987.

————. "Cuerpo/presencia: mujer y estado social en la narrativa argentina durante el proceso militar." *Nuevo texto crítico* 4 (1989): 155–71.

Mattoso, Glauco. *O que é tortura.* São Paulo: Brasiliense, 1984.

Medina, Enrique. *Desde un mundo civilizado.* Buenos Aires: Ediciones Milton, 1987.

————. *The Duke: Memories and Anti-Memories of a Participant in the Repression.* Translated by David William Foster. London: Zed Books, 1985. Originally *El Duke.* Buenos Aires: Milton, 1984.

————. *Las tumbas.* 34th ed. Buenos Aires: Ediciones Milton, 1988. English version as *Las tumbas (The Tombs).* Translated by David William Foster. New York: Garland, 1993.

Méndez-Faith, Teresa. "Sobre el uso y abuso de poder en la producción dramática de Griselda Gambaro." *Revista iberoamericana* 132–33 (1985): 831–41.

Michelson, Peter. *The Aesthetics of Pornography.* New York: Herder and Herder, 1971.

Millett, Kate. *Sexual Politics.* New York: Ballantine, 1970.

Morello-Frosch, Marta. "Biografías fictivas: formas de resistencia y reflexión en la narrativa Argentina reciente." In *Ficción y política: la narrativa Argentina durante el proceso militar,* 60–70. Buenos Aires: Alianza Editorial; Minneapolis: Institute for the Study of Ideologies & Literature, 1987.

Mussell, Kay J. "Gothic Novels." In *Handbook of American Popular Culture*, edited by M. Thomas Inge, 153–69. Westport, Conn.: Greenwood Press, 1978.

Naipaul, V. S. "Argentina: Living with Cruelty." *New York Review of Books*, January 30, 1992.

Ortúzar, Ximena. *Represión y tortura en el Cono Sur*. Mexico City: Editorial Extemporáneos, 1977.

Partnoy, Alicia. *The Little School: Tales of Disappearance, Survival in Argentina*. Translated by Alicia Partnoy, with Lois Athey and Sandra Braunstein. Pittsburgh: Cleis Press, 1986.

Peters, Robert. *The Blood Countess: Erzébet Bathory of Hungary (1560– 1614), a Gothic Horror Poem of Violence and Rage, with Bathory: A Play for Single Performers*. Cherry Valley, N.Y.: Cherry Valley Editions, 1976.

Pizarnik, Alejandra. *La condesa sangrienta*. Buenos Aires: López Crespo Editor, 1976. Originally published in 1971. English version as *The Bloody Countess*, translated by Alberto Manguel, in *Other Fires; Short Fiction by Latin American Women*, edited by Alberto Manguel, 70–87. New York: Charles N. Potter, 1986.

Plotnik, Viviana. "Alegoría y proceso de reorganización nacional: propuesta de una categoría de mediación socio-histórica para el análisis discursivo." In *Fascismo y experiencia literaria: reflexiones para una re-canonización*, edited by Hernán Vidal, 532–77. Minneapolis: Institute for the Study of Ideologies and Literature, Monographic Series of the Society for the Study of Contemporary Hispanic and Lusophone Revolutionary Literatures, 1985.

Praz, Mario. *The Romantic Agony*. 2d ed. Translated by Angus Davidson. New York: Meridian Books, 1956.

Previdi Froelich, Roberto. "América deshecha: el neogrotesco gastronómico y el discurso del fascismo en *La nona* de Roberto M. Cossa." In *Teatro argentino durante el proceso (1976–1983): ensayos críticos—entrevistas*, 131–40. Buenos Aires: Editorial Vinciguerra, 1992.

Radway, Janice A. "Women Read the Romance: The Interaction of Text and Context." *Feminist Studies* 9 (1983): 53–78.

Reati, Fernando. "Literatura Argentina de la 'guerra sucia' el paradigma de espacio invadido." *Texto crítico* 39 (1988): 26–37.

———. *Nombrar lo innombrable: violencia política y novela Argentina, 1975–1985*. Buenos Aires: Editorial Legasa, 1992.

Represión y reconstrucción de una cultura: el caso Argentino. Compiled by Saúl Sosnowski. Buenos Aires: Editorial Universitaria de Buenos Aires, 1988.

Riccio, Alessandra. "Eros y poder en *Informe bajo llave* de Marta Lynch." In *Coloquio internacional: escritura y sexualidad en la literatura hispanoamericana,* 49–60. Madrid: Espiral Hispano Americana, 1990.

Roffé, Reina. *La rompiente.* Buenos Aires: Puntosur Editores, 1987.

Ross, Andrew. "The Popularity of Pornography." In *No Respect: Intellectuals and Popular Culture,* 171–208. New York: Routledge, 1989.

Rostow, Eugene. *Born to Lose: The Gangster Film in America.* New York: Oxford University Press, 1978.

Rouquié, Alain, comp. *Argentina, hoy.* Mexico City: Siglo XXI Editores, 1982.

Running, Thorpe. "Responses to the Politics of Oppression by Poets in Argentina and Chile." *Hispania* 73, no. 1 (1990): 40–49.

Russ, Joanna. *Magic Mommas, Trembling Sisters, Puritains and Perverts: Feminist Essays.* Trumansburg, N.Y.: The Crossing Press, 1985.

Sánchez, Luis Rafael. "Apuntación mínima de lo soez." In *Literature and Popular Culture in the Hispanic World: A Symposium,* edited by Rose S. Minc, 9–14. Gaithersburg, Md.: Ediciones Hispamérica, 1981.

Sarlo, Beatriz. "Política, ideología y figuración literaria." In *Ficción y política: la narrativa argentina durante el proceso militar,* 30–59. Buenos Aires: Alianza Editorial; Minneapolis: Institute for the Study of Ideologies and Literature, 1987.

Sartre, Jean-Paul. *Saint Genet: Actor and Martyr.* Translated by Bernard Frechtman. New York: George Braziller, 1963.

Scarry, Elaine. *The Body in Pain: The Making and Unmaking of the World.* New York: Oxford University Press, 1985.

Sebreli, Juan José. *Los deseos imaginarios del peronismo.* Buenos Aires: Editorial Legasa, 1983.

Shaw, D. L. "Notes on the Presentation of Sexuality in the Modern Spanish-American Novel." *Bulletin of Hispanic Studies* 59 (1982): 275–81.

Silva, Aguinaldo. "Violação: ato sexual ou de poder." In *Sexo e poder,* compiled by Guido Mantega, 157–66. São Paulo: Editora Brasiliense, 1979.

Simpson, John, and Jana Bennett. *The Disappeared: Voices from a Secret War.* London: Robson Books, 1985.

Symons, Donald. *The Evolution of Human Sexuality.* New York: Oxford University Press, 1979.

Teatro Abierto 1981: 21 estrenos argentinos. Buenos Aires: Argentores, 1981.

Theweleit, Klaus. *Male Fantasies.* Translated by Erca Carter and Chris Turner. Minneapolis: University of Minnesota Press, 1987–1989.

Torre, Javier. *Las noches de Maco.* Buenos Aires: Editorial Legasa, 1986.

Torres Molina, Susana. *Extraño juguete.* Prólogos: Ricardo Monti y Eduardo Pavlovsky. Buenos Aires: Editorial Apex, 1978.

La tortura en América Latina. Buenos Aires: CODESEDH, 1987.

Torture in the Eighties: An Amnesty International Report. London: Amnesty International Publications, 1984.

Tschudi, Liliana. "El teatro de Griselda Gambaro." In *Teatro argentino actual,* 88–93. Buenos Aires: Fernando García Cambeiro, 1974.

Verón, Eliseo. "Ideología y comunicación de masas: la semantización de la violencia política." In *Lenguaje y comunicación social,* 133–91. Buenos Aires: Ediciones Nueva Visión, 1976.

Vidal, Hernán. *Dar la vida por la vida: la agrupación chilena de familiares de detenidos desaparecidos (ensayo de antropología simbólica).* Minneapolis: Institute for the Study of Ideologies and Literature, 1982.

———. *Mitología militar chilena: surrealismo desde el superego.* Minneapolis: Institute for the Study of Ideologies and Literature, 1989.

Volek, Bronislava, and Emil Volek. "*Guinea Pigs* and the Czech Novel 'Under Padlock' in the 1970s: From the Modern Absolutism to the Post-Modernist Absolutism." *Rocky Mountain Review of Language and Literature* 37, nos. 1–2 (1983): 20–52.

Volek, Emil. "Summary: Semiotics of Literature under Pressure, Aesthetics and Pragmatics of the Argentine Novel in the 1970s and 1980s." In *The Redemocratization of Argentine Culture, 1983 and Beyond,* edited by David William Foster, 61–63. Tempe: Arizona State University, Center for Latin American Studies, 1989.

Walsh, María Elena. "Desventuras en el jardín-de-infantes." *Clarín* [Buenos Aires], August 16, 1979, "Cultura y Nación," 4.

Woodyard, George W. "The Theatre of the Absurd in Spanish America." *Comparative Drama* 3, no. 3 (1969): 183–92.

Wynia, Gary W. *Argentina: Illusions and Realities.* New York: Holmes and Meier, 1986.

Zagorski, Paul W. "Civil-Military Relations and Argentine Democracy." *Armed Forces and Society* 14 (1988): 407–32.

Zalacaín, Daniel. "El personaje 'fuera del juego' en el teatro de Griselda Gambaro." *Revista de estudios hispánicos* 14, no. 2 (1980): 39–71.

Zayas de Lima, Perla. *Diccionario de autores teatrales argentinos (1950–1990)*. Buenos Aires: Editorial Galerna, 1991.

INDEX